THE GOD BUSINESS

Books by Ignatz Sahula-Dycke

The God Business (Essays)
Alias Kinson (Novel)
The Way to Design (Art Instruction)

THE GOD
BUSINESS

Ignatz Sahula-Dycke

**Polemic Essays About
Religion and Its Effect on
Western Behavior**

EXPOSITION PRESS **NEW YORK**

FIRST EDITION

© 1973 by Ignatz Sahula-Dycke

All rights reserved, including the right of reproduction in whole or in part, in any form or by any means, electronic or mechanical, including photocopying, recording, or by any information storage and retrieval system, without permission in writing from the Publisher. Inquiries should be addressed to Exposition Press, Inc., 50 Jericho Turnpike, Jericho, N. Y. 11753

LIBRARY OF CONGRESS CATALOG CARD NUMBER: 73-86805

ISBN 0-682-47783-4

Manufactured in the United States of America
Published simultaneously in Canada by Transcanada Books

IN ANTICIPATION

Only education emancipated from theistic dogmas can dynamize a moral ethic fit to reconcile the various ethnic strains now populating this planet

CONTENTS

Preface	9
Introduction	15
The Way to an Emancipated Existence	25
How Did We Get That Way?	49
The Empty Promise	54
Thinking versus Believing	60
That Old Bogy, Fear	67
Of Christianist Folly	74
Inquisitiveness	78
"He Died for Our Sins"	82
Of Original Sin	87
The Radio Evangelist	91
Conclusion	96

PREFACE

Sociologists, elder statesmen, jurists, penologists, educators and others, all except clerics, currently agree that only a new morality can prevent the collapse of the top-heavy commercial and technical superstructure of our society. They state the problem but offer no solution—no suggestion as to how this new morality is to be created and its benefits realized. Gone is the time when such people concurred, validly or not, in the view that the problem is resolvable by religious belief. In the existing need, though the religion which once sufficed in such instances is by force of tradition still with us, and here and there is still held to be the answer, the prevailing disregard for its precepts shows it to be anachronistic, powerless. Today's citizen is consequently constrained by his life's inescapable demands to view religion's attempts to ease them as he would the fussing of a senile busybody.

When we consider how importantly religion figured in his existence in the past, that it now means so little to him is almost incredible. But who today worships Ra, Osiris, Zeus, Jupiter, and other deities of now expired civilizations? They're ignored. Today's senior cleric, as aware of this as anyone, views with nostalgia, and apprehension, the people's indifference toward religion. He remembers how easy it once was to engender in the people awe for religious dogmas, and notes that with every scientific advance his work of perpetuating dogmatism is growing more difficult. All that's left of his erstwhile numerous, genuflecting and servile flock is a cadre of people of the older generations, with an ever thinning sprinkle of freshly indoctrinated young, all still taking his religionary promises for holy truth. These people, his loyal supporters, can't for the world comprehend why so many others today are disenchanted with him and the religion's traditional attitude and outlook. But, be sure, he does.

Now although we Westerners as a whole are Christians, and assume in all contingencies that we are wide-awake, religiosity has denatured our personal perceptiveness. Indoctrination affects everyone; and though some more than others, in any case, as I see it, it tends to produce a subnormal consensus. Yet, that each of us indeed harbors a mind of his own becomes evident whenever anyone tries strong-arming us to see things his way. Arrogance of that kind brings us to, makes us once again determined to become sovereignly individual. Were indoctrination not inhibiting our normal judgment, then, even though we'd not be solving our problems the way our dogmatists recommend, we'd solve them as in our more self-reliant days: by detecting their cause and removing it. These days most of our problems result from our trusting that things are as we are being told they are. It was bound to happen; it's only a short step from believing what the parson said to doing what anyone else said. Told by demagogues and hired propagandists that we'd be smart to trust people who said their acuity of vision exceeded our own, we saw in it a chance for shirking our responsibility, and, falling for their dodge, swelled in self-esteem at the cost of deteriorating in conscientious judgment.

By mistrusting our individual judgment, we've little by little over the years also lost confidence in the good sense of joint endeavor. Remiss in this, we are almost entirely depending on George and his magic wand to fix everything for us. All this we had better get busy and correct, for everything now is at loose ends and nothing solved. It's a problem soluble only by our reassuming responsibility. Should we not, we might as well forget all about self-governing ourselves. Indispensable in this is the part of the educator, the statesman, the news media and, above all, the part of the people unreservedly committed to our Declaration and our Constitution's provisions. The educator's part is helping the new and old generations convince themselves that responsible demeanor is rewarded by personal happiness; the statesman's, providing the educator with the opportunity to exert his guidance without interference by sundry selfish interests; the part of the news media, to tell it like it is. Then gears will mesh. But principally important in this is that we begin thinking without bias and prejudice, with our back turned on dogmas.

Every dogma is mere opinion offered in the guise of truth. Dogmas discourage independent ideation and action, making people into virtual puppets responsive to the desires of whoever manipulates the strings. Though decrying dogmas of all kinds, my main objection here is to dogmas of the kind that breed sanctimony, which, inculated by means of ingratiatingly subversive propagandizing, are, as I see it, chiefly responsible for the social bewilderment and agony now plaguing us. Not until we give up our thoughtless devotion to such dogmas here at home, can we justifiably impugn similar dogmatism anywhere else. But most important, our enslavement by baseless opinions of that kind precludes our benefiting from emancipated education.

Were a study of the subjects scheduled in this book's opening essay pursued in our grade and high schools, this would cultivate independent thinking, an incorruptible morality, and a high regard for equity: a triple antidote for most ills of the kind today disrupting our peaceful enjoyment of life. A study like that, encompassing all in the past that mankind has done and still is trying to do about controlling itself—and giving the individual an idea of his importance to it—would lay a firm foundation for a serene outlook. It is worth anyone's implementing, because we do not have to face endless conflict, national and international, once we give up the senseless factional conceits that nowadays as in the past periodically incite it.

Education now remains the lone means of achieving this aim. I'm aware that no matter how good any educational procedure for arriving at unprejudiced ideation might be, it will take time. It can't be done with a crash program in a few months. But hewn to for eight or ten years it would result in our seeing elementary, high school and college students prepared with unbiased minds to cope with problems that, here at home and elsewhere, are extremely anguishing. Most important is that we get the green light and begin.

Ever since 1895 when Durkheim analyzed the theories of Saint-Simon, touching on those of Comte, Thierry, Condorcet, Linguet, Montesquieu and others, sociologists (but very few of our own) have agreed that the Western world's industrialized society will develop a new system of life and a consonant moral code. Were Saint-Simon and the others alive today, I'm sure they'd note that their theories are being translated into at least some action in every corner of our world. Circumstances have been impelling the Westerner toward social equity now for more than a century, and though he still hasn't reached the goal itself, I think he will; but not before he and his fellow workers who actually produce the West's increasing wealth will understand that their respect for outworn dogmas confounds whatever social improvements contemporary circumstances are forcing them to militate for. To succeed fully here, every Westerner would need to be rationally minded, and this the system doesn't afford all an opportunity for, it gaining its authority not from disseminating the truth but from exploiting what the people are ignorant of.

The man in the street would readily turn away from the dogmas were he to delve into the history of social philosophy. But to expect him to undertake that study—in addition to his daily labor—is asking too much. A concise exposition of the most charming of the dogmatic flimflam, explaining how and why today it still victimizes everyone, is a timesaving short-cut on the road to any understanding of the existing problem. That's what this book sets out to do, amplifying it by calling attention to the need for the unbiased dissemination of various other facts now obfuscated by the religionary attitude of our political and educational institutions. By this way deferring to tradition they are helping perpetuate a consensus based on dogmatism and the withholding of information.

Note: The word *Christianism* and similar other appellations appearing throughout the essays refer strictly to the dogmatic religionism visited upon the world by the Council of Nicaea in A.D. 325, that, together with clericalism, everyone nowadays calls Christianity.

THE GOD BUSINESS

INTRODUCTION

Any qualitative analysis of the history of ethics shows that behavioral rules derive from one or the other of two concepts. One sees human nature as good, and the other one evil. My lifelong observation of my fellowman prompts me to speculate that he is a complex creature, his behavior the result of three factors. The first factor enables him to be reasonable; the second, unreasonable; the third makes him a slave to habit. When he is reasonable he is a marvel, constructive and benevolent; when unreasonable he quarrels, destroys and murders; in his habits he displays both reason and unreason in various ratios. But the more reasonably he behaves, the nearer he approaches being ideally humane: a creature deserving to exist.

No one has yet expressed more trenchantly the role education should be playing in our modern society than the Chinese sage Mencius (born 371 B.C.) in the following sentence: *Establish educational institutions for the instruction of the people; the object of them being to illustrate the human relations; when these are roundly portrayed by superiors, kindly feelings will prevail among the people.* A century ago, translators of the Chinese philosophies, savants like Rev. James Legge usually partial to Christianity, quite naturally interpreted those Chinese ethical doctrines to mean that the object of living was virtuous behavior, ignoring in toto their own translations of numerous passages defining in crystal-clear terms their Chinese authors' convictions that the object of virtue was the promotion of a happy existence.

Since none of us know what we were born for, it's pure pretense for anyone to advise us that we were born to be virtuous. This kind of deviation from valid reasoning, outcome of the Judeo-Christian doctrine that man is evil, is commonplace in Western thinking until this day, appearing in the comment we nowadays read and hear about our civil revolt. Only rarely does any one of the current crop of pop scribes and speakers recommend anything for ameliorating the revolt except more and still more of the same dull piety fundamentally responsible for it. Instead of giving their audience rational reasons for comporting themselves ethically, they continue supporting the standard religious dogma commanding those who'd gain after death the reward of God's heaven to behave now as told, or else. They're apparently hopelessly blind to the fact that this anciently droll tomfoolery they sponsor will never do for curing the now widespread major social problem, having previously failed in the instance of minor ones.

Their recommendations testify to a childish faith in the charisma of their religious brainwashing. If the foregoing isn't true, then nothing is but that they're hiring out their talents to authorities avid for rule who, overlooking no sure bets, figure that having religion on their side is safer than having it against them. They're betting on its dogmas. Of course, anyone employing such measures for power doesn't deserve to get or retain it; not because this employment of religion is "improper," but because it is unreasonable. Anyone so inclined has little if any sympathy for the common man and therefore not an inkling of how to emasculate the causes of his existing revolt—an uprising that should be expected to last until the citizenry now engaged in it will no longer have any reason to participate.

The people who recommend religion as a corrective for our problem are no more to blame than all the others who agree with them, including the assembled but silent. All say that religion is in trouble but have no idea why. They're all guilty of not heeding the obvious, that our fix is the outcome of the science-triggered loss of faith in sanctimonious soothsaying and of our failure to replace it with something better. We sorely need that better something because, though all say they abide by Christianity, none take it seriously enough to practice it. And yet, for anyone today, anywhere, to openly criticize its long-propagandized dogmas is to court estrangement and suspicion if not reprisal.

The reason for this is not that people believe, but their lack of understanding *why* they do. This makes bigots of men, whether black, white, yellow, red, or brown of skin. Their bigotry represents a serious obstacle to anyone committed to breaking the grip of superstition on his fellowman. Anyone able to surmount that obstacle is an exception; in our system perhaps only men of art are able to attempt this with little harm done to their material survival and none to their self-respect—the authorities viewing them as visionaries of little consequence in the action.

But whatever the case, our system actually itself sparks the speculation about the relative value to life of its combination of virtue and vice. This prompts some people to become its sharply articulate critics and others its blindly loyal or impecuniously motivated partisans. Yet, in our system, the freedom for speaking one's mind, whether occasionally resulting in a skinned knee or a crisis, makes it preeminent as a practical teacher of reasonableness and benevolence. It encourages hope, and idealism.

It's axiomatic that no matter how people behave there's always a cause. When people misbehave and the cause is removed, or only neutralized, they're on the way to equanimity. Often, when the people of a self-governing nation are crying for justice and not heard, they rebel. For example, when among other matters they want an end put to a war bestializing them, a war their elected representatives nevertheless continue to permit being waged, their inertia points out in them a sad lack of the resolution and determination that go hand in hand with a conscience derivable from a rational morality—a lack they are unaware of.

Practically everything about the way people get along nationally, internationally and racially is affected by the education they receive when young. And more important than anything else at that time is moral guidance. A critical flaw in that guidance appears when the people who glibly discuss the morality of this and the immorality of that are taken by surprise when reminded that none of our schools instruct the young in ethics, and that for centuries the morality of almost the entire Western world has stemmed from religion. Religion's proscriptions, dogmas and ritual, together with the lip service we pay them, constitute what we call our Christian ethic. That ethic is all that served and now is failing to serve the Western people as a moral guide. In all those centuries no nation of the West has taken steps to provide its citizenry with a better guide, a sensible and realistic one, to decency of demeanor.

Though schools of various kinds continue to curricularly support and propagate the religious dogmas once upholding the West's moral attitude, no school engages in *secularly* lecturing on the essentiality of morals; not one explains the benefits of responsibly moral comportment; no teacher dissects what morality is compounded of. From the days of Rome's downfall up to the present everything pertaining to moral ethics has been left to Christian indoctrination, the effectiveness of its dogmatic precepts depending on the clergy's hazardous thesis that God punishes the miscreant. Today even those who in Christendom represent its pillars of belief in God only barely reflect it. Once out of church they bid good-bye to the tenets they attribute to God—tenets therefore useless, and for that reason responsible for most of the tragic events of contemporary times. All this, so malignant, we ignore.

Why has the Christian ethic failed? Why is it still deemed beyond reproach? Why hasn't anyone done something about improving the situation? This book replies to these and other pertinent questions.

The peoples of the various nations and races today bicker, quarrel and at war kill one another only because the moral codes of each and every one of them don't comply with the rest. And even those who tell us they are Christians are at odds due to their religion's doctrinal inconsistencies and its sectarian fragmentation; look at the Irish. Obviously, then, were all the world's peoples to respect the same rational moral standard the world would be a place to enjoy life, not fight it. The ethical precepts for bringing about this sensibly desirable way of life would amply answer the purpose, if they would not simply forbid but *encourage* man to strive for the achievement of goals basically intriguing all humankind. A guide of that kind is not difficult to formulize and its acceptance is as sure as sunrise. The ethic's nonexistence is due to the relatively few people who sense in anything of that kind a danger to their mode of life and/or authority. They're obstructionists of legislative efforts for things ethical, humane—shirking the responsibilities devolving on everyone in proportion to his circumstances and means.

Such realities imperatively demand the establishment of a new point of view on life honoring the principle of human equity. This beneficial kind of outlook is attainable through unbiased public (school) education. But to expect support for it from those now

Introduction

in authority would represent a hope for a miracle which that gentry shows no interest in performing. While this view of the problem is pessimistic, hope for its solution must not be permitted to wane; the need for the education is critical; without it we never will have a moral code yielding universally acceptable results. This will entail our familiarizing the people with the various efforts in history to establish the type of conduct then desired, and explaining to them how and why the character of the precepts employed for this purpose induced conduct that either promoted or impeded public progress and happiness. An outline of the curriculum for public education in this field is suggested in the first essay. Adopted and implemented it would establish the understanding needed for avoiding utter chaos, people multiplying apace and all cleaving now to false and conflicting precepts.

Those who behave decently, telling us they live by the Bible, apparently refer to those of its passages recommending behavior of that kind. But a deceiver, thief, even a murderer can plead just as truly that he abides by it because the Bible spares no praise for actions of that vile kind. The book imposes a heavy load on its reader's judgment, shows no concern about his capability to discriminate between the advisable and inadvisable. The behavior of some Christians is good, of some bad, and of others average. Only a fool would think the Bible makes them so. In this respect the demeanor of the Biblists in no way differs from that of people who say they're guided by the Koran, the Mishnah, the Sutras, or any other religious text. The Bible is the rootstock from which sprang the bole of Christianity and the branches of the dogmas that no longer bear moral results. It's now our task to implant and cultivate something more productive.

That Christian dogmas are of biblical origin is of no consequence; important is that they're well-nigh ignored today, proving once again that respect on the part of one human for the prerogative of another is impossible to achieve by the simple expedient of worshipping God. This has been amply proved by the bloody wars of the past and present, all fought by hosts obeisant toward God or Gods of one or another kind since the dawn of history. Not until man employs rational precepts will he attain the decency and the humble dignity he has ever striven for. Today, when despite their Christian indoctrination you see so many of our young lying, stealing, using drugs, vandalizing, and all with utter abandon—and their elders only shaking their heads over it when not themselves lying to get the young off—will you deny that you are witnessing positive signs of our religious ethicality's terminal shortcomings?

Man is what he is and today behaves as he does because he is an ever changing, evolving entity. He has always been susceptible to ideas of others—his personal progress to an extent ever suffering from this. When for purposes of ruling him the ancients induced him to believe that he had an evil disposition that only his rulers' attention could correct or forgive, he in the acceding became a pawn in the game played by those who recognized his weaknesses a bit earlier than he himself. It made little difference that at that same time benevolent men tried making him perceive that he was a creature essentially good; the number of those who envisioned him as a source of profit to themselves far exceeded those who saw him not as their inferior but their potential equal.

This situation, in which the one attitude opposes the other, has existed in the Western world for many centuries to this day. Here the prime matter to decide isn't which of the two ideas is correct, this being a matter of mere opinion, but which is the more reasonable. It demands no great perspicacity to see that the concept of *evil man* is itself evil, and the concept of *good man* essentially good. This makes it impossible to deny that anything structured on the premise of human depravity is fundamentally unsound. Anything of that kind contradicts everything that man, left to himself, would instinctively conceive himself to be. Those who keep on dinning into man's ears that he is evil will soon have him believing it, turning a potentially good man into a thoroughgoing rascal. Like it or not, such is Western moralism, an offshoot of modern Christianity's dogmas, with all its behavioral tenets either predicated on or in their observance affected by the concept that human nature is evil.

Hardly anything that happens in the West is unaffected by this scandalously erroneous concept, belief in which is constantly nurtured by the clergy—a procedure staunchly approved of by the laic authorities who, of habit resulting from indoctrination, consider it pure wisdom and that way continue its abetment. The evil in this is therefore perceived only here and there, and, being only a drop in the bucket, has little or no effect upon public behavior. Doesn't this show beyond doubt that the evil rests in the cleric's successful merchandising of this premise as fact—he managing it by dint of unrelenting repetition? And to crown all this he avers himself the agent of God, able to forgive man's evil. This leads to another question: On what grounds is the cleric able to absolve the wayward—he being one of the selfsame breed his kind dubs evil?

Sprung from such ground, is our ragged morality surprising? There's talk at this writing that Congress is mulling over the legalizing of prayer in our public schools. What next—conscripted worship? As long as our clericalism supports this insane situation and abets such unreason, our moral standards will remain largely ineffective and our comportment continue unimproved. Our children should be taught that ethical behavior is of direct benefit to their life, instead of being prompted to believe themselves sinners. What has manacled our reasoning? What are we trying to evade; what are we pushing off on God? The personal responsibility for our stupid actions?

For many years after I learned to read I looked for books that would substantiate that there existed the just God about whom I'd already been told so much. Looking, I read all kinds, including volume after volume of Christian zeal expressed in words of subtle persuasion, all devoted to the business of religious indoctrination; but evidence? None. In my search I nevertheless found things rewarding all my trouble: the Analects of Confucius and the Works of Mencius—and no mention by those two of God and His punishment of the wayward. But for them and for ironic or humorous but cogent rejections of our Judeo-Christian dogmatism by Voltaire, Ingersoll, and Twain which I read in my teens and, later, forceful words in similar vein by Russell and Shaw, I might have given in to overwhelming odds, resigned myself to my early brainwashing and remained a victim of Christian dogmatism.

I read Bertrand Russell for the first time in 1918—his *A Free Man's Worship*. From then on I looked forward to and when available relished everything of his that came to my attention. His ardent drive to overcome the religious bias that deadens reasonableness is in philosophic annals without parallel. Possibly I'm imputing to myself some of his observations about religiosity in remarking that God is an invention long employed for mollifying man's atavistic fears and for controlling his galvanic reactions to life's realities. Russell's contrareligious speculations are like a draft of cool fresh air vitalizing the prejudicially polluted stuff we all breathe in the world of today. And though the world is slowly discarding many old concepts for having proved false, it stands guilty of many times rejecting valid ones. Russell's *Why I Am Not a Christian* will tempt even a rabid bigot to experiment with reasoning. A paragon of everything humane, a sworn enemy of sham, Bertrand Russell was dedicated to hosting his fellowman with the satisfying fare of clearly reasonable conclusions.

As for my efforts, I've written as I have in order to explain that a renaissance in reasoning is gradually making inroads into the West's penchant for clericalism, and that the nonsense in religious dogmas is primarily responsible for the disdain shown by the new generations for traditional behavior, whether good or bad. I've also written to show why in the West religious indoctrination of almost every child is considered the thing that must be done, and the consequences of this unreasonable disregard of each passing generation for the prerogatives of the new. I've described the way that all this can be ameliorated by education without prohibiting anyone from *privately* worshipping God as and if he so pleases.

I've met with no evidence that God exists, but I have no quarrel with the rank and file of believers in whose midst I've lived all my life. Some of them have on occasion and at times to my surprise tried to excuse my heresy by saying that I don't really mean all I say. My protestations availed little; believers don't seem to understand how anyone can appear decent without a Psalter in hand. It is a tragedy of a kind in this era that such religious misconceptions prompt so many of our people to reject educational steps which couldn't but help enliven and heighten everyone's appreciation for responsibly moral conduct. People who deem such steps antireligious just don't realize that spiritual fulfillment is impossible without prior attention paid the humane.

During this writing I've often reflected that I should stick to my palette and canvas instead of intruding where, as in my younger days I was told, only experts are qualified to speak. But when I see how religious twaddle misdirects and devitalizes the incipiently potent minds of the children and adults around me, my blood goes cold and my canvas runs a poor second to words. I hope my work here will point out to all concerned that time devoted to phantasms of religion could be utilized to better advantage in speculations about the wonders bundled up in, say, a hummingbird or a fragrant flower.

THE WAY TO AN EMANCIPATED EXISTENCE

I

The history of man's behavior and his dealings with others would make a book only very few of whose pages wouldn't mention bloodshed. This is made plain in many books, including the Bible, which records the activities of only a minor segment of the many that constitute the human race. This record of man's behavior nevertheless reveals that for at least a few thousand years he has been trying to take steps encouraging the student of human behavior to hope that humankind is tending away from rank animalism toward reason and benevolence in dealing with the multiple problems of its survival.

But much yet remains that man must do before earning forgiveness for the trail of misery he has left wherever in the past and current times we've watched him go. Anyone when informed about mankind's muddled attempts to turn from conflict to amity is that way to an extent qualified to judge the potency of the concepts employed for that purpose in his immediate community and society, and enabled to estimate the rate of man's progress toward the elusive goal of reciprocity—the goal he must soon reach or for lack of ethicality suffer genocide.

But reaching the goal is no simple matter. Often in history the methods man thought would improve his creature status have been little short of grotesque. Take our own case today. When friendly border and overseas nations tell us that our national ethic is the dollar, we must admit they're not entirely unjustified when saying so, for nearly everything we do we seem to appreciate more keenly the more it amounts to in terms of dollars. Despite all this, that the dollar is our ethic is no longer true. At least not true now. The 90 percent tax bracket is something that relatively only few of us actually aspire to—even though many think they'd not mind being in it. I incline to believe that at this time our ethic is technology—it is little short now of being viewed as our Deity. There's no evidence contradicting that, mistakenly or not, instead of a God of sorts, technology is what we are depending on to save us from extinction.

Nevertheless, practically everyone who has devoted some thought to the matter concludes that our idolatry of technology—its accomplishments usually presented in terms of billions of GNP dollars—needs counterbalancing by a new and self-redeeming kind of rationally genuine aspiration, a matter not as easily concluded as wished. We face here a problem of major proportions because aspiration when untempered by reason often departs from sanity—and we are a good way from being entirely sane.

The present era, especially here in the USA, is notable for its wide dissemination of information. Much of this power could serve for breeding a healthy aspirational attitude were everyone prepared to understand why and how it would directly and indirectly benefit him. It's a matter for education. During the past quarter century this lack of understanding has imposed on us—in addition to the Christian ethic we started out with—the materialistic ethic we now have, the two of them amounting to a mismating in which neither of their discrete principles is serving us as an ethic properly should. It's a stalemate, as a result of which whatever of any import that in the past we might have applied to the cultivation of rational understanding and aspiration, we've for lack of preparation directed to the satisfying of material desire.

This now affects consensus, especially and regrettably the outlook of those in authority who should be initiating steps for correcting the existing situation but still are refusing to do so. Their refusal thus condones religious bias, furthers racial prejudice, and results in all sorts of makeshifts intended for patching up what has turned out to be a botched-up situation. Knuckling under to dogmatic edicts has clouded our perception, interfered with everyone's recognition of obvious facts, and precluded when not delayed the changes and adjustments so necessary for the pacification of the societal turmoil both here at home and abroad.

The existing discord testifies how irreconcilably we all are divided into two camps each differing in outlook from the other. The majority of us still worship superstitions come down from the past—our minority wants to live guided by the results of evidentially substantiated observation, reasoning and analysis. The discord thus simmers down to the difference between those of us who defer to mere opinion and those of us who rely on solid facts. Many of those of the majority would readily embrace the outlook of the minority were they not dissuaded from it by all those who craftily benefit from the majority's susceptibility to religious claims, political shibboleths, and educational taboos—all examples of contemporarily respected dogmatism. Encouragingly, many signs today seem to indicate that this way of subduing sane reasoning is nearing a deserved end.

Within the majority, many think the existing social upheaval to be the malicious work of malcontents who have little if any reason to complain. Were the people who believe this to probe the situation impartially, they'd find most of it ascribable to their own and their neighbors' unconsciously acquired bias: outcome of their exposure to outdated dogmas and to opinions presenting but one side of the issue. It is this biased attitude the dissident minorities are militating against and want changed because it precludes equity.

Though this reveals the problem to be anything but simple, the clerical fraternity—whose opinions most of the people of the majority take more or less seriously—as always holds that the solution rests in the peoples' reversion to faith in an unprovable hypothesis: God. Another but more militant group within the majority sees an answer in the inhumane expedient of dosing the dissident with gas, bayonets, and gunpowder. Both of these suggested courses of action exemplify dogmatism at work treating the symptoms of the trouble instead of its cause.

Lincoln said that dogmas of the quiet past were inadequate for the stormy present of his time. This statement, made more than a century ago, fits our present situation like a glove. Our trust in old dogmas today keeps alive old misconceptions and prejudices—and our indifference about it withholds from education the necessary freedom to disseminate facts which, made known, would lead to rectifying the injustices responsible for the existing difficulties. There's still hope that education will be given the green light to teach everyone the factual significance of morality: why moral behavior is desirable, how moral as well as immoral conduct affects everyone's life and, last and most important—of what at a given time moral behavior may or may not be compounded. Until everyone is that way helped to *convince himself* how indispensable to his well-being decent conduct is, all other measures will be of little avail, and our troubles will only keep on growing and multiplying.

To this day, if and when morality as a subject appeared in any public school or college curriculum, it was treated only superficially because the authorities ever took for granted that religious upbringing with its threat that God punishes the sinner was ample for producing in each new generation an adequate reaction conducive to passable behavior. But year after year, especially after World War I, the pastor's flock has been less and less responsive to his threats of God's displeasure with sin. Now, in view of this religionistic failure, urgent need exists for a morality erected not upon dogmas but upon reason. A morality of that quality, countermanding no creed, would be universally acceptable and would more than compensate for the fiasco of today's religionism in its role of moral preceptor.

Today's world buzzes with propaganda—most and best of it at the command of two great rival forces: Christianism and Communism. Though no need exists in this polemic to discuss their relative significance or merit, these two isms, differing in origin and ideation, are exactly alike in having one overriding defect. Both are despotic oligarchies, existing because most of the people comply with the dogmas of one or the other in fear of the punishment these isms threaten to inflict, each in its way, upon the dissident. For that reason, were no matter which of the two in the end to prevail, humanity would still come out loser. So the discord between the isms themselves, and within the various national, ethnic, and racial groups forming their populace is actually the result of yearning, on the part of dissident minorities within them, to enjoy uncensored expression of their thinking, and to be free to seek for a way to sanity and equity in human affairs. Christianism and Communism will for once agree in rejecting the previous statement. This is understandable because each proclaims itself the one true champion of deliverance, notwithstanding that neither one will admit it resembles the other.

Nevertheless, no little in Communism stems from its founders' previous Christian indoctrination and consequent understanding of the goals attainable by the application of fear, and as true is it that much in Christianity derives from anciently despotic authoritarianism, which today's West calls oppressive tactics when its rival employs it. Punishable in both bailiwicks is openly adverse criticism of any opinions held by the oligarchy. Regimented Christianism, stepchild of Christ's theosophy, owes its origin to the zealous efforts of Saul of Tarsus (St. Paul) and the political shrewdness of the Roman emperor Constantine. Authoritarian Communism, its roots in the theories of Marx and Engels, was shaped by Lenin's policies toward underdeveloped countries into a close semblance of its rival. Today each of those isms constitutes a politico-religious cult.

Though each cult considers the other a poisonous wellspring, both exist in their current form as a result of political and ideational urgency. Strange though it may seem, both were enabled to develop as they did because in the days of their emergence thought and its expression were largely *un*suppressed. Had free expression at that time been restrained in the way they themselves are now restraining it, chances are good that neither one of them would be here today. Also, though each one constantly praises the virtues of its godhead, both of them obtain credence for whatever dogma they wish to establish, by extolling it as the holy truth—and secure the people's lasting belief in it by imposing it on them as early in life as possible.

Should we never have anything better than these two isms to choose between, the big question is: in which of those two areas will free thought first gain the encouragement enabling people to find the best way to a life of peace and plenty? Whichever of the two will first support free thought will that way gain the ascendancy and, no matter which one, its peoples' mistrust of old dogmas will be the first sign of the ensuing change. Such changes take time but are inevitable.

Contributors to an awakening of this kind are various minority leaders whose straight thinking even when censored does some good because people are adept at reading between the lines. Here in the USA this has been jarring out of complacency many of the people long in control of education: those who endow educational facilities as well as those who administer them. As to the students of all races and nations, their uprising is in most instances not to be taken for an attempt to do away with a system established by their elders, but as a protest against an institutionalism fascinated by technological acumen but blind to its societal responsibilities. All this presages a change in the world's mores long overdue, leading to an improvement in international and racial relations. This could turn out to be the genesis of a third, truly humane, ideology.

The preservation of order in any society always devolves on its upholding, but retaining in amenable condition, the moral rules helping make living pleasant for its people. In the old days, in a prospering nation at peace with all others, this was no great problem. Today, the agitation, dissent, and the wars racking the world attest that religiously precepted morality falls far short of the desired goal—a problem which unattended to is apt to lead us more deeply into trouble rather than out of it. This wouldn't have materialized for yet some time had the clergy taken forfending steps—anticipating that in this scientific age its precepts, because based on the fear of God, would be increasingly ignored. It failed to do so. When people saw that The Bomb represented a greater threat to their peace of mind than religion's Hell, it followed that religion waned as a moral force. This now shifts to the civil authorities the chief responsibility for improving the people's moral standing, a move the clergy is hoping to prevent, saying religion is reviving, soon to have a greater effectiveness than ever before.

Organized religionism, aware of being in crisis, is doing everything it can to present a gracious image of itself, hoping that way to win the people's loyalty and, through it, control over their actions. Our entire clerical community is diligently trying to regain its former standing. It still is lent a deferential ear in high political, educational, and even military councils; commands fabulous material resources; enlisted in its service are experts in oratory, history, languages and idiom, medicine, art, literature, science, etc.—not to mention astute politicos, shrewd propagandists, sophistic philologers, and masters of dissimulative debate. Just what this worldwide cartel is going to resort to in its try at extricating itself from its difficulties will be interesting to watch. It is a truly historic struggle between the dogmatic and the rational.

Today, no mind can avoid the shrapnel of religious propaganda. There was a time when sanity of mind could be secured by going home and locking the door. Now, all mediums, especially radio and television, penetrate the walls of that once impregnable bastion, and big guns, commandeered for convincing the timid that in church is their last chance to save the existing system and themselves, wham away. This attack, much resembling offensives that always before prevailed, will probably fail, aiming at a humanity much better informed than any before. But the outcome is still uncertain because no one sponsors the lone thing that can secure here at least a draw: a non-theistic, realistic, reasonable guidance to a morality that could and would make for and sustain a satisfyingly equitable life for all.

The religious taboos today still passing for moral standards only keep people from having a superior guide to humane behavior. Currently going on is exactly what led to the collapse of every previous society. Each of them derived its character and strength from a set of maxims that upon failing caused the culture to disintegrate. *Morals* are to the intellect what a *compass* is to the sailor—a guide. In a society like ours, tending toward technocracy, should its sense of right not keep up with its attainments in technology, the intellect bereft of direction will because of it revert into simple animal cunning, nothing more. This consideration the West doesn't seem to want to, but should, assign first place to on its agenda of business deserving serious attention and earliest possible educative implementation.

Were anyone born ten thousand years ago still alive today, he having spent all those centuries travelling the globe, in that period he would have witnessed the behavior of various nations and races in different places and climes, generation after generation from ancientry to the present. His speculations about it all would have led him to consider factual that life on earth began because the sun gives light and heat, and once that star stops shining that life here will end. An observer like that would be fit to render a trustworthy opinion about humanity. But one thing would puzzle him: why the world's people failed to realize that their prevailing belief in the very same superstitions they believed in millennia before is the chief reason why to this day they haven't done away with quarrels and wars. The confirmed realist seldom views life through rose-colored glasses but accepts it, good or bad, on the basis of evidence; never on terms outlined long ago by men who reasoned that the human would rather listen to soothing fables than grapple with life's sometimes stubborn facts.

Only by distinguishing between the real and the unreal is anyone able to improve his own life. Those who take the long view sometimes succeed in improving life for future generations but again only because they clearly foresee the outcome of the realities existing in their time. As concerning relations between states, and races, their dogmas and ideation differing, nothing but a mutually realistic recognition of existing issues will ever obviate serious friction between races and, between nations, resentment that on past occasions terminated in the miseries of a shooting war.

Anyone desiring to alleviate humanity's existing ills and prevent the onset of more will be more apt to succeed if guided by facts. Depending on dogmas here amounts to courting defeat. The cleric preaches "Take your problem to God and He will solve it." Can the cleric explain why the prayers of untold millions are never answered? When the realist asks, "Who created God?" the priest palters: that question, irritatingly ambiguous, is now often put to him. Today all the West is in turmoil because so many in it no longer fully trust him, and those who still do are ever more difficult to manage. The people who believe his "God watches over you" must be deemed the ingenuous kind who, using it as a crutch, thereby indicate their vulnerability to demagogic exploitation, whether open or shut to discussion of the various reasons liable to upset their belief.

There must be thousands who, ignoring promises of that kind because finding no substantiation of them, are forced—because in their daily life they have to deal with the many who blindly believe in such things—to pay them lip service. Within the indoctrinated majority are people half ready to junk their belief but, loath to take the step, they spend their lives one day soothed by their waning faith and the next day irritated by their mounting doubts, remaining schizophrenic because no one leads them out of the legend's labyrinth. Numerous others carry on the comedy, their brainwashing preventing them from admitting to themselves how absurd has been their lifelong payment to it of token homage. This is not to say that within a rationally oriented society a mentally overwrought individual couldn't benefit from occasionally speculating about an unverifiable Elysium.

II

Everyone's life is affected by the pattern cut of his childhood beliefs. Nothing with which our Western civilization today madly attempts to correct its ills will do as much good as would our getting rid of the habit of leading our young to accept as truth the multitude of theistic dogmas and similarly irrational nonsense which, because of our sentimental regard for tradition, we deem indispensable for the continuance of our erstwhile hallowed but now disintegrating morale. Even were this vicious habit of ours to endure a while longer, we should remember that we've never attempted anything that would or could stop or, at least, neutralize it. Were we to try and in either case succeed, we'd be treading the solid ground of an enviably sane outlook.

The question isn't why our young won't accept what we've tried to impose on them, but what exists in it that they can confidently trust. How can they or anyone in their predicament arrive at any viable conclusions about life if the discriminative segment of their thinking potential is disequilibrated by misbeliefs introduced to them by our high regard for the implausible? The religionistic axiom that man collects a reward for respecting and observing "God's laws" can satisfy only those who have all they need or more.

Many well-off people sooner or later conclude that true happiness is to be realized but in peace of mind: the net result of treating one's fellow man with genuine consideration and material generosity. They practice what they preach and feel good as a result. They don't do it from fear of God's punishment; they've emancipated themselves from superstition. The position in life enjoyed by such folk is something the underprivileged work and sweat for but hardly ever experience; it's obvious that it can't be attained by anyone in dire need.

But for the cliché, popular with the greedy for conscience-salving, that some people are damned to stay poor, there'd be few people facing want and starvation. It is mainly because the majority still either conforms to or complies with dogmatically engendered views of that variety, that the new, irrepressible generations and their sympathizers grow ever more disenchanted and insurrective. Should they be censured for calling our attention to the need everywhere for fair play? The danger in demeaning the young or bodily assaulting them is that almost anything that opposes a system indifferent to their hopes appears preferable to them. Consequently, anyone who has a gripe and is aware of these feelings of the young, is perfuming his particular ism for them to embrace. All such people are hoping that the young will pull the chestnuts out of the fire for them. The average citizen, baffled by this scene, then votes for the doctor who promises he has a sure cure for it: the politico with a sugar-coated version of the same old dogmatism that started all the trouble.

People ask what this world is coming to when more important is to know what the world is running away from. Running, probably, from signs indicating that coming up is a change calling for some sharp decisions and hard work. This could turn out to be great fun despite even exceedingly tough work were the cleric only to stop dinning into our ears that our hopes of attaining a full measure of happiness on earth are mostly vain, and how preferable to this vale of tears is the Kingdom of Heaven. Whoever first loosed this bit of religious sophistry upon an unsuspecting world must have been a hyperascetic to think that anyone could be cheered up by it.

Christianity's ideation is extremely lachrymose. One period of its history is notable for having spawned thousands of drawings, paintings, mosaics, murals, polychromed sculptures and illustrated tomes all depicting the goriest possible suffering. The Stations of the Cross, a series of pictures to be seen in many churches, and portraying the few incidents of but one day, have this way taken on an importance in the minds of the worshippers out of all proportion to the teaching Christ is said to have aimed at the promotion of human brotherhood. It is undeniable that all this, including the crucifix with its blood-flecked image, evokes a variety of commiseration in the viewer, but to no purpose that anyone except a religious zealot or a missionary would call salutary, or imperative for establishing a humane outlook. Things of this kind date back to the days when fair play was considered a sign of weakness and held in contempt by most of humankind.

Should Christianity under the same name still be here a century hence, it will more than likely then bear little resemblance to its anemic self of today. In this era of The Bomb it will have to change and assume the job of fending for man by coming to grips with anything threatening to destroy him. This will mean switching from the governing side of the aisle to the side of the governed, a move promoting some material good that could gain it forgiveness for its erstwhile fussing about afterlife. Should it try to get by, as now and in the past, with but its humdrum ministering in day-to-day life to the dying Christian, and on the bloody battlefield of war to Christians of opposing sides killing one another—the latter testifying to its utter failure as a teacher—it will only be the final confession of its utter uselessness in any exigency.

Today, should any religion at all be needed, it simply must take into account the sophisticated world of the present—a world and people as different from yesterday's as the megalopolis is from the cave. This a few radical and enterprising clerics are already trying on their own to implement, and being dubbed rebellious for it. But most of them are still in the same ancient rut Constantine's chariot cut in history when taking their infant religion from Nicaea via Byzantium to Rome. The cleric will more than probably be the last remaining on the bandwagon for the fable about heaven and such but—fragmented by sectarianism as his religion is, and he pledged to uphold its dogmas—is no longer a teacher qualified to render consequential assistance in the prevailing outcry against social inequities.

A conscientious teacher encourages his students to question all aspects of existence and to analyze the value of everything employed in it for promoting a balanced society. He will not conceal pertinent facts known to thoughtful adults like himself. This only happens when the teacher isn't pressured by his superiors to resort to a sentimentally or politically colored explanation of the subject. This kind of mind control in education—say the authorities—is advisable because unnecessary criticism of traditional practices might generate in the students disrespect toward our free society! This rocky road is now being traveled by every forthright teacher, but the religious preceptor is in no way inhibited by the authorities because they benefit from the very matters about which these future citizens can be kept disinterested or uninformed by means of dogmatic twaddle.

Every cleric must be aware that something now missing is needed to keep his theistic dogmatism from collapsing. If nothing else, the steadily declining patronage of his business ought to awaken him to the fact that he should be delivering much more to contemporaneous life than only his mollifying sermon. Were he to interest himself in facts, don denim overalls and take a look at his dogmatism from below where most of the people are, he might for the rest of his life join the crowd suffering from it. That would be something everybody could applaud him for. But today he still extols the questionable virtues of religious trivia for the same reason that steel and other things are manufactured: his work is approved of and considered useful by those in power who want things kept running on the same old tracks. This is the part he plays in our way of life; but viewing it as he would like us to, as an endeavor he calls God's work, will not solve our existing problems.

III

It's a moot question to what extent today's charged-up Westernism benefits from traditional clericalism: of its support of the clergy. We know that the moral garb which the thread of religionism held together for so long is coming apart at the seams, and that while we are busy mending away at one place it is coming apart in another. It happened before in other cultures, and was repeated often enough for us to have learned a lesson from it. One after another all religions came into existence for serving man's designs if not needs and, failing in this, each succumbed to be replaced by another more befitting doctrine. For better or worse our religious ideation is still with us, just like the poor old lady who can't go anywhere unless someone charitably pushes her there in her wheelchair.

Many people, partial to their religion, will ruffle at many of my remarks, especially that both Christianist and Communist doctrines stand on and arise from the fear of punishment, and that they foment fervid partisanship resulting in bigotry, suspicion, and enmity toward all who disagree with their dictums. It's almost certain that these folk, because of my statements, will feel exactly that way toward me, therein proving how true is what has been said. If Christian, they'll probably be concerned with only the part of my remarks indicting Christianism and, if Communist, the other way.

I, mainly interested in the effect such dogmas have upon the West, think it proper to point out that in opposing me, the Christian at one and the same time opposes one of his religion's sacrosanct dogmas: that God punishes infractions of His (actually the priests') commandments. Also pointed out should be that ever since prehistoric times the responsibility for effecting command over humanity was by its chiefs and rulers delegated to religion. All religions are based on the priests' invention of God and His wrath—effectiveness of this concept resting in the frail human's superstitious fear that this God will punish him. No God ever threatened anyone—always it was His self-appointed middleman the priest who did. It is beyond doubt that religion employs the God concept for the exclusive control of man; otherwise the priests could explain why God doesn't punish any of His other creatures whenever they engage in doing exactly the same thing that in the instance of the human the priests call sinning. Since no evidence pertaining to this and other similar matters has ever come to light, all "authority" on the subject of God's justice must be deemed pure and simple dogmatism. Be that as it may, punishment is always cruel, whether God's, the teacher's, father's, Hitler's or Stalin's—cruelty and punishment are one and the same.

The attitude of the religionist has undergone perceptible change in recent years; this modified outlook of his connotes that freethinking is penetrating the hard crust of dogmatism to an appreciable depth. It is becoming unseemly to attribute cruelty to God; even the priest is getting uppity about it. This weak variety of dissent, though dissent it is, testifies that our clericalism can't prevent some improvement in the West's antediluvian outlook. It wouldn't surprise me too much upon opening my newspaper were it reporting that an ecumenical council deprived God of His prerogative to punish transgressors—and that in the Bible any mention of His ire was due to its mistranslation by some ancient and overzealous bibliolater. Were this to happen, the old Bible would look like it was shot full of holes.

It is unrealistic, but not a few people think that without religion moral behavior and respect for law would disappear. Right now we have very little of either, but lots of churches. Good and bad, and right and wrong are values of behavior, not of religion. As values, the two are of account to law. Within the scope of law, right and wrong are words symbolizing behavior that community opinion at one or another time either approves or disapproves of —calling the good *moral,* and the bad *immoral.* Laws are the outcome of community consensus, their observance preserving peaceably ordered relationships within the community's territory. All this sounds simple, and would be, were dogmatism not constantly to interfere when need for change appears in it. But the cleric, indoctrinated and trained to demand a piece of the action, is confident that he has better answers to life's perplexities than any unchasubled mortal. Any time the stakes are worthwhile he is sure to be there with the Bible for authority.

Were people in their youth not religiously, but rationally, indoctrinated, any community could get along better without clerical ministrations than with them. In the USA this is almost unthinkable today despite all the talk about the separation in government of the church and the state. Just the same, now and again even here one or another event rekindles hope that the people are emerging from the mire of clerically sustained and politically exploited dogmas. The existing necessity for doing away with public reliance upon dogmas, both religious and secular, now obstructing the way to a realistic morality, much resembles the need for doing away with ignorance about sex, the latter a matter which public opinion long wouldn't open its eyes to, but now is beginning to turn over for correction to public school education. The latter matter was hard opposed by the religionists, over whose objections reason, finally, and fortunately for everyone, prevailed.

IV

History describes how civilizations come and go. Our Western kind, too—call it System, Establishment or whatever—will one day go, not to be saved by Art, Religion, Industry, ABM, Integration, The Pill, Antipollution, Labor or Diplomacy; nor by a trip to Mars or Pluto. The most that any one or all of that array can contribute to its life will only put off for a time our day of reckoning. In the current exigency, wherein Education alone can signally help but hasn't been permitted by public opinion to so much as sharpen a pencil toward it, a little humor might be in order, but only for calling attention to the absurdity of the condition now victimizing us. Blue in the face from choking on dogmas, there's hope still left that we'll survive if we'll get whacked on the back and cough them up—and start breathing normally as we should.

To people interested in their own and world affairs, and by the tireless news media constantly reminded of this era's insanity, life represents a hopeless mess. Such people nowadays wish for a life more orderly, more enjoyable, and meaningful. Many of them think our system badly needs improvement, but can't say exactly how this should be done, being too busy making ends meet to give the problem the required attention. Those who've gained this or that by adjusting to the daily grind might suspect anything new as a danger to their hard-won estate; but, were moral stability to prevail, it would safeguard everyone and especially people of their reasoning kind. Our way of life—and in it everything that now controls us—needs reappraising.

Ideas for improving man's existence get nowhere until the intelligent segment of the public demands what one or another such idea suggests. My proposal belongs in the educational category, so its explanation should be the responsibility of the executive educator. I mention later on why I think he has steered clear of doing it. But at this date most of our educators say that the curricula of their devising are excellent and that when, as in recent days, they've been or are criticized by the community for falling short of the goal, it is only because the critics sympathize too much with the young who are neither experienced enough nor qualified to understand their worthiness.

The situation is much like the plight of the shepherd who, to save time going home in a storm, wants his flock to go over the mountain, but his dog from habit keeps on pushing the flock around its base. Our educators, bless them, are like that faithful dog. Granted, here and there they've adopted "progressive" courses, and the instructors—many of whom like the system no better than do the students—now teach that way; but all this still aims at the same old goal of conformity; and by no imaginable means at the students' intellectual emancipation. There is no valid reason for conduct of this kind. It rests in our fear of the facts of life, and in our belief that faith in ancient fables will keep us from making serious mistakes.

Most of our recent educational ameliorants are missing their mark because the students are more intelligent than they are being given credit for. Their mass behavior speaks louder than any words, and reveals that their preschool upbringing and subsequent elementary education saw them off to a bad start long before they entered high school or the university. It's commendable that now, in school or out, they are doing the best they can, on their own, to get out from under the load of psychic trivia their elders imposed on them in the traditionally approved way.

Life is never much of a problem once anyone attains a balance in it between his personal requirements and the demands of his environment. School is where the young have ever been told they'd get the most help toward it. In itself, the rebellion of today's new generations—of all nations and complexions—is nothing new; the young of previous generations just weren't so perceptive nor so vociferous about it. They were a meeker breed because in their day the prevailing system's rewards for suffering regimentation were relatively more equitable.

Nothing is perfect, certainly not the increasingly complicated system that helped us become the envy of the world materially. But in that system, as I see it, the agency now impeding our realization of intellective morality has been clericalism. It seems to me that any reasoning individual should be able to understand that all responsibility for a soundly effective morality, in a system so scientifically geared as ours, ought not to be religion's. Had it been education's, as it should have been, and long ago, the current difficulties would have been forestalled. No known religion is able to promote a morality fit to hold together the fabric of a culture representative of the contributions of many races and nations—an ethic that can be a guide to all and no less to one than another.

We read and hear a good deal nowadays about methods for correcting social ills: Sensitivity Training, Human Relations Training, Open Admissions to Universities, Ethnic Integration, The Ultimate Religion, etcetera. But the fact overlooked by nearly everybody—probably because it is diffused throughout everything that we see every day—is that all these methods and possible others to come are but attempts to repair faults in the makeup of people that could never have appeared had they been started off, from childhood, in a more reasonable way. If we will refuse to see the good sense in giving up our old ways of cramming our children with religious pap before they're fit to digest it, we will never see an end to the existing pandemonium.

Children are nothing but young adults; we try to confine their minds within the limits of moldering concepts, try to make them conform to our ways, instead of giving them rein for showing us the world of the future, the one they'll willy-nilly have to build all by themselves. Yet, in the intellectual freedom this way denied them rests the sole hope for our culture's necessary unfoldment. Today's world—this day's—is not the world of only last week's, not even the world of yesterday; it is the duty of the grownup to equip the child with rational tools for coping with today's lightning-fast changeableness. That done, we can relax—confident that the new generations and those to arrive will do better than up to now have we. That's all, and the best, that anyone can possibly do.

V

In previous paragraphs I've tried to make clear why dogmatism should be considered the prime enemy of intellectual progress, the progress toward sanity of conduct between individuals, within the community, the nation, and the entire globe. Were anyone today as ignorant as many were when in Palestine Christ preached his doctrine of human brotherhood, it would be novel to hear proclaimed that people should treat one another as themselves. Today we know that it was nothing new; Confucius, hoping for human equity, said the same thing six hundred years before Christ, and the record tells us this was preceptorial in Egypt millennia before.

It shows how slowly the world takes to heart admonitions that if followed could make everyone in the world a whole lot happier than he is today. That concise maxim makes good sense. It is fully rational. It is just about all that needs to be said on the subject of human equity. The Council of Nicaea, in A.D. 325, relegated that admonition—together with other precepts that Christ hoped (and which the Council should have recognized) would promote realistically humane behavior—into relative insignificance by labeling poor, long-dead Jesus as the "Son of God," that way fabricating an attractive religious showcase filled with items reported of his life and crucifixion. It attracted buyers; but I've already covered how their sanctimonious ideation has even since those early days permeated the Western world—interfered in the rest of it—and made extremely difficult the solution of our domestic problems, let alone the coexistence of nations and races.

Today, when practically everyone in the West trusts in assorted dogmas of the various Christian sects, it's sad that the solution still depends on the leeway these prejudiced people will need to give to secular education that alone—by giving the new generations a rationally uninhibited outlook—is capable of providing it. We have never before given our young an opportunity for an unbiased attitude, but it is something they deserve to get. They are now groping for it and, in their way, demanding it. It is due them, and only teachers dedicated to intellectual freedom can help them attain it. But no teacher will be able to help them if we manacle him with our sanctimony, something that the other two-thirds of the world does not accept as rational.

When dogmas hold sway, who will sponsor the educative, morally restorative regimen today representing the lone cure for the frustrations of the West? All past attempts in this direction have failed to overcome the blandishments of three negative factors:

1. *Religious Bias.* Most of the people of the West take for granted that religiosity and morality are one and the same. This popular belief prevails because, in keeping with tradition, it was instilled in them during their formative years. As a result, nearly everyone is to some extent prejudiced, and therefore suspicious of anything, no matter how rational, appearing to threaten what his indoctrination induces him to believe is sacrosanct. This side effect of religiosity is responsible for the mediocre consensus enabling the demagogue to manipulate education to suit his purposes—a situation responsible for keeping the West's intellective level far below the level of its technology.

2. *Few Sponsors.* The educators, and those who endow education who've already perceived or are beginning to see the necessity for a secularly curricular approach toward morality, are so few in number as to not have any appreciable effect on the opinion of the reactionary majority. No realist among those few will expect any educational departure to gain quick or easy approval. The majority of education's old guard and their supporters, because of their religious partiality, will not welcome any duties they now deem the responsibility of religion and the clergy. Committed to clericalism, at least upon first consideration they'll take any such move to represent interference in religious affairs if not rank iconoclasm.

3. *Political Wariness.* It's obvious that any legislator, when asked to pass judgment upon an educational program of this kind, will be cautious. He will not be likely to forget how prejudiced are the people who vote for him.

Despite this triad of negatives, the study of morality should be initiated in grade school and continued through high school. By the end of the last year of high, the student would be fully conversant with morality, and thus immensely better prepared than nowadays he is to embark with an open mind upon the courses of study offered to him by the various college and university curricula. Up until college years, then, the teacher would help the student to think about and analyze the following subjects:

a. Moral conduct means responsible behavior.

b. Mankind's search for moral guidance, and what all religions and each of them contributed here.

c. The part of moral conduct in ancient and modern life.

d. Although all people are created equal, they aren't motivated alike.

e. The sources of human motivations and their significance.

f. How moral ethics guide and control human desires and urges.

g. Hammurabi Code; Akhenaton's Reforms; Justinian Code, outgrowth of Hellenism; Magna Carta; U.S. Constitution; Code Napoleon; Russian and Chinese Marxian Manifestos.

h. The considerations involved in the terms *right* and *wrong*.

i. Being ideally moral amounts to being in step with the basis of life.

j. Why upholding moral conduct is beneficial to the individual.

k. How personal conduct affects the individual, the community, the nation, and the world.

Had the individuals of the last three generations been made aware, by a study of this kind, of their responsibility to one another, I dare say the resulting moral tone would have precluded the selfish attitude that brought on the crisis of hard drugs, criminality, racism, and pollution today forcing us to take belated action. Every one of those and similarly vexing problems arose from our indisposition to cultivate a rationally moral consciousness, a result of the general susceptibility to the propaganda of the religious interests.

It is normal to expect that anything of this kind will meet opposition from the Churches because they'll see it as an anti-clerical move begging for public approval. Seeing a threat in it to the social standing, deserved and undeserved, that their organization, ritual and propaganda for so long enabled them to enjoy, they'll almost certainly say they've been teaching all that for centuries. Blind to their shortcomings due to the lack of concerted opposition, they of course will not realize how harmful to rational thinking has been their dogmatism.

For example: our theologian says that God's laws are self-evident, though he constantly attends to their explanation, and in various ways. He tells us that any moral code devised by man for guiding human conduct is inferior to God's, but conveniently forgets that mortals like himself formulated everything he presents as God's word. He preaches that Christian philosophy is superior to the secular variety, but finds no part of the reasoning which supports religious dogmatism adequate for a conclusive demonstration of his claims; especially irritating is his reference to the Bible as the conclusive authority.

He propagates the tenet that God the perfect Creator created man, but constantly dins in man's ears how imperfect is man, and that man must come to God to be forgiven his imperfections: and doesn't seem to realize that every priest is cast in the mold he calls imperfect—and therefore should not be taken any more seriously than any other mortal when he intones what all is true about God. He moralizes that man should do this and that, while disparaging man-devised ethics as a poor guide to exemplary human behavior. He asks his listeners to believe that Christianity is a superior philosophy, though in attempting to convince us he evades all rules pertaining to philosophy. He says that followers of any but a Christian system of morality thereby indicate a tendency to part from God, and that trusting in such a system is immoral, the while he trusts the man-devised legal code which guarantees him the right of free speech whereby he expresses his dubious claims.

I'll leave all conclusions about these few examples of his reasoning to the reader, though I'll grant he, the theologian, is a clever man—and remarkable besides, the remarkable thing being how rarely his preaching is challenged.

The impeding factor about the way morality is inculcated in the West is that it is done haphazardly. For almost seventeen centuries it has been in the hands of the Churches that to this day *have not been held accountable* for its lack of success. In such a situation nobody can be sure what level of outlook the people are attaining to. In one section the morality might be high, in another low. Nobody is able to say exactly, because no responsible program exists for it—nothing but religionism is offered to the people by way of a guide. A possibly beneficial religionism might be one in which the cleric assumed the rags of common humanity and mixed, incognito, with the underprivileged. But even then by reason of its unprovable claims about God it would remain an activity apart from any kind of rationally estimable reality. One way or another, at this writing, in a culture whose capsule passengers while circling the moon have intoned passages from Genesis into the loudspeakers of radio and television, we should expect some spirited tussling over the right and wrong ways of attaining a better moral tone than the one we have now.

Though surveys indicate that the USA has the highest percentage of churchgoers in the Christian world, ever since World War I our people have expressed in their conduct not Christianity but an ideation more resembling eudemonism, in that the majority are contented only because in the Land of the Free they feel able to attain the kind of gratification they aim for so long as willing to exchange work for it. It is also true that after almost two hundred years of independence the people here by no means display definite signs of ethos, of comportment such as would enable anyone to see them as a homogeneous entity. The country remains a sputtering melting pot. An incontrovertible indication of the split in our public opinion is that some of the people praise, and some criticize the system for one and the same reason: because the clearly documented promise of equal opportunity for all is *not* being impartially implemented.

The day will come when indifference to minority needs will disappear and all will share more equitably than now. That day we will display national ethos. The people could be imparted recognizable character now through education. Given insight via education, the collective individual would then to a much greater degree than presently realize how important is his personal outlook and his ensuing behavior—and begin to understand that he contributes this way to his country's standing within the world's family of nations and races. But today the average Westerner connects whatever he knows about moral ideals and his propensity to aspire with his religion because he was from childhood reared to see it in no other way—and then left at sea to make for shore as best he could.

The insurrection within our society is an intellectual one; it reveals how man's unquenchable hopes and irrepressible desires for improving his lot arouse him to the necessity for distinguishing between fact and fable. The various minorities are fully aware now that the big obstacle they've to overcome is the majority's indifference to inequities. Obviously, the minorities' behavior shows them to have lost confidence in the religious dogma that God ever provides, or they'd not have taken the matter into their own hands.

This is a revolt that no police officer, soldier, magistrate, or cleric, is equal to putting down; this has been tried innumerable times before without success. The application of threats and force might for a time dampen it, but it will always flare up again only to burn brighter and hotter. Only a broadly humane outlook, derivable from the people's understanding of the elements comprising ideal comportment, will ever be able to quell it. The study of morality recommended here and leading to it would conform with our tacit code upholding the separation of church from state, and nowise prevent anyone from privately worshiping God in any way he pleased.

We the people behave as we do and are what we are because of the precepts we do or don't follow. The current social upheaval reveals the flaws that exist in our evaluation of life, and is trying to tell us that our sentimental regard for antique dogmas has blinded us, that it is keeping us from seeing things in their true perspective. Our behavior reflects the extent to which we've departed from the rational concepts of impartial justice that impelled our Fathers to these shores. We are every day now pressured to defer to the very brand of dogmatism that for centuries has kept most of the people of the Old World disenfranchised and all of Europe in turmoil. History testifies that the governments of all those nations have consistently supported the clerically devised dogma that God will provide, it serving to engender in the people patience, hope, and belief that deliverance, though ever abeyant, was at hand. It was the European people's disgust with this and other empty promises that, during the two hundred years before our Civil War, made them view the New World's much freer people with envy, and convinced the Europeans that in revolt was their only hope.

In the century following, most of the significant happenings on our liberated shores took place because their initiators refused to let the Old World's dogmatic ideation affect their aspirations. Whoever now believes that those same old dogmas, in this or any other day, represent anything more than a soporific, is unheeding of the times—is of the same temper as those who in the past failed to prevent the collapse of gloried empires—and therewith invites the progressive dissolution of our own and the entire Western civilization.

HOW DID WE GET THAT WAY?

Anyone falling prey to a bad habit sooner or later finds it prudent to make amends. How much longer it will take before the Western world begins to come to its senses and make amends is an interesting question. The West is being victimized by a vicious habit: its self-righteous opinion of itself; the view sourcing from the religiously engendered supposition of most of its people that Western concepts and actions are to a substantial extent guided by God, making them deserving of respect by the rest of the world. It's a delusion, a mental disease worse than any plague on record, and always involving needless suffering and bloodshed.

In our US for example, nearly everyone from generation to generation has ascribed the country's well-being to the "good start" given it by the pious Pilgrims, the while forgetting that the Pilgrims sailed primarily because they were fugitives: targets of religious hatred fomented by "God's and the King's" Church of England. Before they sailed they asked God's blessings; on landing they thanked Him. Of the 18 wives who sailed, by spring 14 died. That fall, after a bumper crop, the little band set aside a day of Thanksgiving to God. If Massasoit thanked the Western Christian's God for these uninvited guests, the historians forgot to mention it. This adventure, like every other one of its kind, is marked by either a warped sense of justice or a disregard for their God's command against stealing. On what grounds, I wonder, did these pious people deem themselves entitled to appropriate the territory they never saw before? Well, what besides self-righteousness?

Our confusing, doctrinaire Christian religiosity sometimes produces bizarre results. In 1861, for instance, a Pennsylvania cleric proposed that were something done publicly recognizing God's omnipotence, God would favor the North in its war against the South. I feel confident that the same thing was proposed by one or another biblist on the other side, but isn't being mentioned, the South having lost. However, as a result of the Northern cleric's inspiration, after 1864 most of our coinage bears the words *In God We Trust*. The cleric's idea was a propaganda coup outdoing the best of today's Madison Avenue cunning—God would be advertised every time anyone pulled a coin out of his pocket. This bit of self-righteousness climaxed as recently as 1955 when Congress ordered the motto to appear on all our paper money in addition to the coinage.

Starting with Jamestown in 1607, the country grew in this kind of atmosphere to giant size. But who can authoritatively deny that we grew on despite the religious prejudice, witch-hunting and bigotry spotting the record of our bygone and even recent days? Joe McCarthy the Self-Righteous was in full swing less than twenty years ago. The rest of the world judges us by our record. Were we to see ourselves as others do, it could get us over our so sanctimoniously false sense of being God's do-gooders. Our crusade in Southeast Asia turned out to be a full-blown tragedy commanding us to take another look at ourselves in the mirror. If we won't learn from that, then Jefferson's vision of a great country of truly free people on these shores will be only a memory.

Self-righteousness and sanctimoniousness are hypocrisies attending any doctrine that establishes beliefs and behavior contrary to fully sane and rational thinking. Whenever those former two manifest, they are proofs of any such doctrine's fallaciousness. In the sphere of the religions they are no recent phenomenon. The Roman Church was disregarding its own precepts, and Christ's too, for a thousand years before the Reformation. Not very long afterwards the same thing was happening in most of the Protestant sects. Nowadays most of the Christian church officials are guilty of the very things Christ was against: lust for power, hatred, collusion and other vices, all of them hallmarks of the relatively few people who in every generation are unable to resist the impulses of avarice and selfishness. Their example affects adversely the decently disposed people of the entire globe. Though much that's favorable can be said about religion's past and present activities, it isn't enough to outbalance the harm religion has done. Christ's ideas, most of them good, play only a minor part in the Christian ethic of today.

The churchgoing individual's participation in worship and allied activities is the outcome of his indoctrination when he was very young and emotionally susceptible to it. When he continues in it after maturity, it's mainly because he has been so intensively brainwashed that independent thinking, which could enable him to forget theism, is almost impossible. Further, the thread of religion interlaces, and has become so much a part of, so many social activities as to make the thought of departing from the religion a decision of major proportions. So, once indoctrinated, most such people remain captive within the limited confines of their childhood's religiously induced fantasies. Nevertheless, even these people can be reached and shown the difference that exists between fantasy and reality. Anyone who venerates religious concepts and dogmas won't be able to do that all by himself, nor will anyone like that be fit to teach it. Religious beliefs keep the human thinking apparatus operating on a level considerably below that of reality. No matter how rational any religion appears at first glance, it always takes its addict back to superstition.

We can depend on one thing about the cleric. Trained as he is in all the appeals to superstition, and in the semantic trickery which keeps alive the myths which, when believed, deter free thinking, he will not slacken his efforts. And you'll be much nearer right if you'll conclude that he is more a man of the world than a "man of God." Almost inevitably, however, a few years after he takes his priestly vows, he comes to realize that although the religious dogmas he sponsors are mostly pure nonsense, they're also the merchandise offered by a well-established and widely respected business organization, and that when he gets buyers for them it benefits himself and all those others who, like himself, are employees of the God Business. He has learned that the business exists because the average human looks for the easy way out from under responsibility, notably responsibility to and for himself. At this juncture is the cleric's moment of truth. Vows or no vows he now either leaves the clerical ranks, or for better or worse stays to make the most of man's superstitious weaknesses.

Once man comes to realize that his difficulties won't disappear by his doing what he is told, especially not when obeying those chiefly responsible for the problems, then, acting rationally on his own, he will be on the road to much greater contentment and happiness than anything of that kind promised him by religion.

But, as things stand, Western man keeps on piddling away a good part of his precious life in deference to religious commands. Were it possible, say a century ago, to arrange matters so as to have him religious only during the first half of his life, and for the rest of it have him independent and rationally freethinking, the day when the world's peoples will live without fear and oppression might already be here. But, still superstitious, he cringes at the cleric's any mention of the word *God*. He therefore fails to see that he would be a lot closer to true salvation once he realized that his religious addiction is a sure sign of his possession of the gift of aspiration, easily employable for his personal development and for the benefit of his fellowmen and environment.

Most of us don't realize that religious indoctrination does serious and almost permanent harm to our young. If we did, we'd start them out—as soon as they begin asking questions—to distinguish between make-believe and reality; there are many ways, some better than others, but any of them better than enslavement by superstition. I think it criminal when anyone feeds a child fantasy accompanied by assurances of its indisputable verity. Such a person is destroying the child's genetic aptitude for reasoning. Once this is done it is difficult to restore. A case in point occurred a year or two ago when the Catholic Church attempted to retract or correct mumbo-jumbo which long before that time took root as a belief about St. Christopher and others. Believe it or not, the flock just wouldn't have it: St. Christopher medals are being minted and are as popular as ever, "safeguarding" the traveler, and the driver on the streets and highways, just as effectively as before.

Considering the fealty so amply demonstrated here by the believers, it's interesting to speculate about what might happen were the Church to disavow everything else of fantastic character that it (and other sects) promise their believers. The brass of the sundry religious sects nowadays employs every modern facility for disseminating religious superstitions and as well, of course, the way it was done in the days of the Roman catacombs: through the gathering of the flock. The pastor of today still urges the flock to his church where, when they are nicely bunched in pews, he bombards them with precatory words. He does it of habit, and they are there of habit; he repeating the selfsame homilies for the selfsame reasons as have his kind now for many centuries and, as before so now, with no results other than the selfsame misunderstandings among the Christian nations and, tragically, the selfsame bloody and insane wars.

Just about all that anyone who isn't asleep is able to remember of all the sermonizing is that Jehovah stands ready to wreak his wrath upon anyone who disobeys the preacher and doesn't come to listen once again next Sunday. For nearly seventeen centuries the gullible have been this way bamboozled into believing that God was watching their every move, and that God would be no end disturbed were his commands taken lightly; the commands, naturally, relayed to the listeners by the priests, and the believers' compliance with the commands useful for whatever the priests happened to have in mind.

Those who control the Christian masses aren't likely to soften toward anything threatening religious dogmas until forced to do it. The cleric guards dogmatism for its being the source of his authority, such as it is. He and the dogmas would have all the world tightly manacled were it possible. Dogmatic doctrines change only *after* their erstwhile believers, having glimpsed this or that through the fog of dissimulation, threaten to turn apostate. These days the hierarchs are relenting but, be sure, only the bit enough to keep their flocks in hand. Religion rarely leads; after it indoctrinates it tends, and then mostly to its mundane, selfish interests. All this, and more, has made us the way we are today.

THE EMPTY PROMISE

It is difficult to surmise exactly what today's Westerner believes in *and respects*. The only way for anyone to penetrate the situation is to keep an eye on how this complex entity conducts himself in everyday life. Numerous signs indicate that he no longer takes his religion as seriously as did his predecessors. His religion's dogmas no longer intimidate him the way the cleric would like. The demands of contemporary life have forced him to be more critical and inquisitive than people were a generation or two ago. He is beginning to question the validity of religious "truths" and the integrity and intentions of those who direct the Churches. This shows him to be moving toward intellectual maturity at a greater pace than at any time in history. These and other questions he asks are important for they are clues to the intelligence quotient of our times, and because Western civilization will disintegrate unless it produce realistically oriented citizens in greater volume than heretofore.

Why the Westerner says he is a Christian is no mystery. It's a habit that was foisted upon him when he was a child, and was done by adults through whom he came into the world. Those adults, when they themselves were children were treated the same way by their progenitors, and so ad infinitum. Thus everyone, throughout his life, hears religion's persisting claim that it has everything to help man become contented. Yet the Christian remains the least contented of men. If this last is untrue, why, then, are the Western people so at odds with themselves and one another? And why, today, is the West in such insane turmoil? For no other reason but that its people want the contentment which all their life religion promised them but didn't deliver. Disappointed and distressed, they are asking their civil authorities to provide it. The authorities now reply that the people can have it by doing this or that which, if the people follow instructions, will in the end completely deprive them of their liberty.

But the thing that will replace religious promises, deliver contentment, and enable the people to remain free, is readily available. It only requires that the people rid themselves of the blindfold of

The Empty Promise

the superstitious religious beliefs preventing them from perceiving the verities of life: the charms of existence. That Western peoples will eventually do this is inevitable. Already great numbers of them are beginning to realize that Christianity's negative doctrine is only a variety of fantasy: a psychic palliative. This has been recognized by people of religious rank for centuries, usually resulting in measures that improved the doctrine and returned it to favor. Rifts of this character didn't reach serious proportions in the West until A.D. 1382 (more on this later).

When even the churchmen dissent, it's easy to understand why at times the believers do, and why, today, the cleric's once nicely tractable flock is partly insurrective. I think the cleric understands why it's happening even better than the rebelling layman. I'm sure he would be a lot happier were he able to forget that he does; no salesman enjoys seeing his customers deserting him. That's why so many clerics are leaving the profession for fields where equivalent effort is more rewarding and satisfying. And the cleric who stays on is no longer the symbol of religion, respected by laity, that of recent memory he was. He knows it but can't help himself. His preceptors who indoctrinated him to uphold the religion's banner were men whom he'd now only partly dare to trust; their reactionary outlook left him vulnerable; the answers they taught him to give to perplexing questions are no more effective today than a pea-shooter against a battleship. And the inquisitive young, searching for solid facts to support their aspirations? The religious patter so effective over the many past generations leaves them cold.

I suppose the honest working cleric deserves a modicum of respect, but his job, today, is just about the least desirable to seek and hold of all available. It happens every time anything or anybody goes static. There *are* a few steps that, taken by religion, must be deemed progressive, but most of these the religion was by political or social circumstances forced to take; and for every one of these it would be easy to name dozens that were obstructive.

Organized Christianity's skill in opportunism equals if not exceeds anything of that kind in politics. After the death of Christ, the early preachers of the religion, names still honored today for their religious zeal, were more interested in the success of their preaching than in what the Bible reports Christ said. Organized Christianity dates from the year of the Nicene Council in A.D. 325, but long before then we hear that Saul of Tarsus (St. Paul) was preaching his own version of Christ's words and, on top of that, to populations whose conversion—if Matthew 10:5 and 6 is to be trusted—Christ specifically prohibited. Whether Saul was aware of this isn't important in view of the words in Matthew 28:19, to my mind representing a bit of opportunistic interpolation in Matthew's alleged text, making it appear that Christ pronounced those words *after* his cold body was taken down from the cross and *after* it disappeared from his burial tomb.

Important is that the foundations of today's Christianism laid in Nicaea were the outcome of Saul's missionary activities. Although Christ, while alive, said his teachings were for the exclusive benefit of his own people, not for Gentiles, his failure to convince his own that he was Messiah seems to reveal why—so soon after Christ's demise—Saul took the Gospel across the Mediterranean (no buyers for it back home) and why these and other of Christ's admonishments were so abruptly being disregarded by those who, above all, should have been taking Christ at his word. This variety of behavior, which the religious potentate ameliorates by describing it as *apostolic initiative,* studs the pages of Christian archives ever since that time.

More of St. Paul's kind of initiative went to work in Nicaea when a group of power-conscious potentates promulgated that Christ was the divine son of God; and their decision has stood up, though many times under fire, until today. In the group was the Patriarch of Alexandria: Arius, who bitterly opposed this and other related encyclicals. He was outvoted. Why the Council was assembled is clearly obvious: Rome then needed a religion more effective for controlling the people than the Roman one then in decline. The Council was assembled by order of Emperor Constantine who, seeing that the burgeoning new religion might emerge a popular victor over the still-venerated Gods of Rome, played both sides from the middle: tacitly worshipping the Roman Deities until baptized on his deathbed by Eusebius, Bishop and ecclesiastical historian of Caesarea. Nevertheless, ever since then, Constantine has been held in high esteem by the hierarchs of Christianity. A few years later Christianity was proclaimed Rome's official religion, and Rome's old Deities declared pagan. The new religion held the vast empire together until the sacking of Rome, its capital city, by the Goth: Alaric, in A.D. 410. Recovering, it was sacked once again in 455, this time by Genseric the Vandal.

This capsule review of early Christian history testifies that the religious hierarchs' talent in politics goes a long way back. Today, it view of the existing Pope's views on married life, can you disbelieve, were oligarchs of this stamp in command of power such as they exercised in the middle years of the Christian era (with their own armies to enforce their excursions of fancy, when they arbitrarily defined the boundaries of nations, decided who would rule in Europe as Emperor), that we wouldn't see a repetition of the same tragically senseless conduct on their part? Protests against arrogant churchly authority were heard in those days just as they are today, some of them from the lips of men of high rank clerically, all without avail.

The oligarchy of Christendom was first-confronted by inner revolt near the end of the fourteenth century, its adversary the person of John Wycliffe, translator of the Bible into English, who, disgusted with the behavior of the fat, rich clergy (rich from gratuities and alms), asked Parliament to deprive the clergy of its privilege to hold property.

Only thirty years later, Wycliffe's disciple, Jan Hus, accused of heresy, having been granted safe conduct from Prague to Constance by the Rome-crowned Emperor Sigismund, found, on arriving, that the Emperor, that honorable "Defender of Christianity" (pressured by the Romish oligarchs to whom he owed his title), had reneged on his promise; Hus was turned over to the Ecclesiastic Council and was burned at the stake by it in A.D. 1415.

Christianity is far from holy; it sins relatively more than does any individual. Christianity sometimes repents, of course, but usually too late for it to do its victims good, as in the case of Joan of Arc, who was burned at the stake in 1431 (a delayed outcome of being sentenced to life imprisonment in 1430) but whose sentence was revoked in 1456, she then dead twenty-five years! She was later canonized as Saint, believe it or not, by the same Christianity that didn't move a finger to prevent her execution. She was sentenced for witchcraft, for disregarding parental admonishments, for wearing male attire and for heresy. Excellent reasons all.

Savonarola, who protested against the power and luxurious living of the ecclesiastic fraternity, also was incinerated at the stake in Italy in 1498, for heresy. These are only a few of the individuals who paid with their lives for opposing the power of organized Christianity, whose record is stained with almost unimaginably inhuman misconduct. All this was ceremonially perpetrated in the name of God and Christ, but actually to ensure that the temporal power of the Christian oligarchy would continue undiminished and unrestrained.

We view with horror and revulsion all that Hitler and his henchmen perpetrated by way of mass murders and worse, and because of this we disclaim and have outlawed Nazism. But do we disclaim Christianity, whose record over the centuries is as bloody, as senseless and reproachable—the responsibility for which is on men who considered themselves (or wanted to be known as) men of God? Records of thousands upon thousands going to their early deaths because of dissent make grisly reading—as revolting as anything in Hitler's day. Over a thousand Huguenot dissenters hanged in France in 1560. Between 1480 and 1780, 300,000 women (1,000 per year) were executed, usually by burning at the stake, some buried alive, for witchcraft and consorting with the devil! These people and recorded and unrecorded multitudes of others all died because they tried to show their fellowman a way to truth, or because they ignored or disregarded the despotic edicts of the Christianity of their day.

It would seem that any deep, one-track participation in Christianity is an affliction manifesting in brain-lag and confusion, terminating in an addiction to vengeance. Certainly Christianity as practiced in the past, and as known and practiced today by almost a billion adherents, is a very perplexing quantity. Those who've studied it don't see it as the Christian sees it. To him it represents goodness and, because this attitude of subservience was instilled

The Empty Promise

in him before he learned how to think, he believes his belonging makes him decent. This is his delusion. Christianity is like a fading mirage which, though it engendered hope in men for reciprocity for some centuries, is doomed to expire unless it somehow undergoes marked change. This is reasonable to assume because the ethics which originally made it welcome are largely ignored today when not wholly contravened, making it known the world over as the religion of the nations that say one thing and do the opposite. Within the Christianity of today, a handful of cold ashes represents what's left of the precepts Christ hoped would make the world better than he found it.

THINKING VERSUS BELIEVING

What should anyone believe nowadays? A fair answer would be: anything he would lay his life down for. And what to disbelieve? Almost anything that looks attractive. It's a mad world we live in: no one thinks anything is worth dying for, but can name any number of things he'd trade his integrity for. The entire world, especially our Western one, is so full of attractive gadgets that its people think they can't do without, that lying, cheating, duplicity, bribery, kickback, and other shining virtues are the order of the day; all of them the result of desire gone wild. It's enough to make any halfway sane individual turn away in disgust from the entire stupid mess which, nowadays, is touted as the most advanced civilization in all history.

What has become of honor, honesty; of the people whom the words *Know Thyself* once entranced? What accounts for the disappearance of the daydreaming idealists, the honest craftsmen? Why all talk but no conversation about the mysteries of existence, love, music, painting, sculpture, the starry cosmos, literature, and other subjects about which, as often happened, the participants had but little empiric knowledge but a lot of curiosity? What is it that has made us believe that we have all the answers and now only need somebody else to do the work? This state of mind probably represents the most acute crisis ever faced by Western man, most of it ascribable to his long-persevering, perversive and, by now, almost systemic irrationality.

Harsh words but true; because the crisis will persist until he reverts to rationality. Through no fault really his own he has got himself in a trap which will be a good deal harder to get out of than in. Getting out depends not on his thinking but on his making a change in what, up to now, he has been *believing* instead of thinking. But so long as he keeps on worrying more about what the Soviets and Maoists are about to do to him, instead of what the Christianists and Theists have done and are doing to him, the chances of his escaping the trap are very slim. He's trapped good and solid; no one can help him but he himself; he's in a fix demanding he use his head, or perish.

Thinking versus Believing 61

In this crisis—which resulted from the West's intellectual and creative progress during the past few centuries, *and to an important extent from its seventeen-centuries-old belief in Nicene Christianity's divine afflatus*—all the Gods of Christendom and Pagandom combined will be of no help. Any belief in a God or Gods, wherever it exists, is nothing but a belief in a fantastic invention that, lacking confirming evidence, is to all purposes a lie. All of us know who the two who got us here were, but what the purpose is of our being here and what, if anything, all our struggling and fussing actually means is a puzzle as old as humanity that each of us, once here, should be permitted to try solving by himself.

The search for the answer is as old as the puzzle itself, is supermaterial, dynamizes inspiration, and constitutes the most important of the conjecturable reasons for living. It is what life is all about: is its essence. This fact is largely ignored by the great majority of the West's people because their instinctive desire for the search has for centuries been suppressed by religion's false solution, which it presents as an incontrovertible fact. The people who believe it look no further. This is unfortunate because of its side effect: an evil more insidious than the ersatz answer. It actually divides the people into two opposed groups: those whom the religious answer satisfies, and those who, rejecting the pseudo-answer, persevere in searching for an answer that would satisfy their rationalism.

This division, this difference existing between the two groups, is the trap from which it is imperative that Western people escape. Thus divided, and with the majority of them depending on God to solve their problems, the rational thinking of the minority produces only a slight effect when necessity exists that any serious problem similar to the existing crisis be solved. This suits the demagogue to a T, and now constitutes both the cause of the present national and international intransigence throughout the West, as well as the obstacle in the way of its entirely possible satisfactory solution. This notwithstanding, it must be solved, and will be, though not before the people return to an appreciation of life on a basis of rationality and fact, and not on religion. This isn't about to happen although it's quite possible—were only half of the believers induced to accept that the religious and the political are separate and independent entities. If that happened, the rational minority together with half of the entire majority would thereupon constitute a consensus sufficient for making the needed change.

The majority's delusion that religion's answers to various riddles of existence fill the bill is due to the cleric's cultivation of the people's susceptivity to superstitious fantasying. A wide variety of delusions, God, hell, and the rest, have this way gained the respect and obedience of unenlightened masses ever since the dawn of history. Old records tell us that comets, eclipses of the sun and the moon, boreal and austral auroras and other natural phenomena were viewed with forebodings and terror as omens auguring all sorts of imagined cataclysms. Nowadays they're still magnificent, but are regarded as the wondrous workings of immutable forces supporting, not threatening, all life. This is the realistic outlook, untainted by superstition; but enough superstition is still around, all of it causing trouble. That so many people, in this enlightened day, still take stock in religious dogmas—some of which are no more factual than that the moon is made of green cheese, is due to the prevailing situation in public school education which ignores the fact that a difference exists between reality and fantasy. This omission encourages dogmatism in giving free rein to beliefs in which most of the students have already been parentally or clerically initiated.

Considering what is everywhere to be seen of temples, pagodas, synagogues, and churches; of domes, steeples, minarets and towers; it's undeniable that those who take religion at its word are in the driver's seat, and that way forcing the rationally minded to tolerate all kinds of irritating driving. Though thus inconvenienced, from the rational minority have nevertheless come most of the contributions making life ever more enjoyable. Realistic thinking is slowly gaining the favor of the masses, this undoubtedly a source of encouragement to the few nearly apostate clerics who, through their progressive *societal* work, are hoping to convince their superiors that the means and the power of Christianity's wide-

Thinking versus Believing

spread organization should be employed for the cultivation of a rationally self-reliant, not a genuflecting, humanity. This would mean that a few idealistic though realistically minded clerics could move a Pope or some other religious nabob to depart from his titled and exalted duties as guardian of organized religion's original purpose. Anyone familiar with Nicene Christianity's purpose considers the hopes of such clerics noble, but by no stretch of his imagination realizable; could you believe that a leopard can change his spots?

In but one generation we would see a tremendous increase in the numbers of rational people were the majority's establishmentarian religiosity to stop interfering with the natural aptitude for thinking characterizing the normal child. All human young are born inquisitive, are natural searchers. Almost as soon as the child starts talking it begins to cerebrate, and wants to know where it came from and, not long after, why it was born. It is beginning to think but not yet able to differentiate between fact and fiction. Later, when its questions come like a hailstorm, should its elders reply to them in terms of the Bible—Genesis, Jesus, etc.—then, for all we know, one of the world's potentially brilliant minds has been started on its way to regimented mental mediocrity that, in a dozen years or so, transforms the child into only another adult conformable to the dictates of his dogmatic environment. Children aren't simple bags of bones, flesh and blood; they have instinct, and feelings advising them of anything contrary to the sense of well-being.

Children who—while growing and being religiously indoctrinated—rebel against the religious routine then being imposed on them, are in that way showing that they've been endowed with common sense and with exceptional aptitude for reasoning. Tots like that aren't able—yet—to say why the religious routine: those solemn, somewhat awesome goings on provoke them; they only *sense* them as contrary to their instincts. This happens in the instance of half or so of Western children suffering indoctrination.

But does anyone bother to protest against this savagely pernicious routine? Has anyone ever bothered to understand it from the child's viewpoint? I'll guess not even one in a million of the parents and the elders, for they themselves were similarly made the victims of the system. As a consequence, when starting the child out in life this way, they are stupidly and smugly sure they're doing the right thing. They're doing wrong, however; in the light of our existing knowledge their behavior is inexcusable. And so is any public or private educational institution that aids in this injuriously irrational brainwashing.

We should be making every effort to hasten the day when every child will be protected from it until it reaches at least its twelfth year. By then, even were our public schools to be no better than today's, but were to include schooling in ethics, the child would there and at home have learned well the benefits of doing right and the penalties of wrong. Knowledge of the difference between right and wrong already existed thousands of years before the appearance of Christianity; it isn't something religious, or new.

Parents who nowadays are bringing up their children to understand the difference between the effects of right and wrong—but without any fear of the spectre of Christianity's vengeful God—this way raising the general level of rational morality, deserve everyone's thanks. Were such people not to have a penchant for facts, and were they not opposed to the worship of superstitious concepts, the rest of humanity would forever stay in the same rut of enslavement by dogmas and ignorance. Even at very worst, the thinking of the rationalists induces the others to change to another rut; the change offering fresh possibilities for the improvement of everybody's day-to-day affairs.

The rational people attend first of all to the needs of their time and its people; this indicating them to be at odds with any doctrine preaching that everyone's fealty belongs first to its dogmas. This old dogmatic viewpoint is irresponsible: today's world needs a more effective prescription for curing its various ills than the salve compounded of unreason and dogmas. In the recently more amenable past we generally benefitted more from our instinctive sense of right than from the religion which indoctrinated us to thank God for every success; but failed to tell us whom to blame for every honest effort that failed. This variety of dogmatism, instead of cultivating the development of responsibility, sets an example encouraging its evasion.

The religion is always making promises which, when broken,

Thinking versus Believing

we hear is the will of God. Very often the believer, seeing the sham succeed, decides to take a flyer at it himself; it can't be much of an infraction, after all, if God's own religion is doing it. This kind of behavior, demeaning one of the basic principles of moral ethics, has over the years resulted in the general moral callousness which today makes the Westerner deservingly distrusted and suspected of trickery by the people of the rest of the globe. Opposition to deceit is naturally instinctive, is fully rational, and not of religious origin; but hard to marshal by anyone who has been made morally irrational by religious brainwashing. Right or wrong, the self-styled Christian's deceitful behavior stems from his indecision: half of it resulting from his cynicism toward his religion's alluring promises, and half from his believing them.

Christianity's deceitful promise of immortality which the religion tells man he can have, provided that he obeys clerical commands, is the most consummate artifice of all ever devised. Nearly everyone unthinkingly imagines he'd like living eternally. But the one puzzling and discouraging thing about it is that it first of all entails dying, which the religion is unable to prevent, but which the religion ought to get busy doing away with because it is an unnecessary step. Could religion ever succeed in this, in a short time there'd be signs reading *Standing Room Only* all over the globe: a disturbing thought to dwell upon.

We've all known deceitful traders who are regular churchgoers. As sure as the sun that will rise tomorrow, there's something about that kind of behavior that's wrong. Either the religion doesn't mind the cheating done by believers like the trader, or, despite all the religious taboos against cheating, the people pay little serious attention to it. Since this is a trifle self-contradictory, let's ask a few questions enabling us to find out of what the discrepancy consists. The questions follow.

1. Why does the cheater keep on saying he is a Christian?
2. Why doesn't the cheater reform?
3. Is the religion cheating in saying its doctrine is reformative?
4. Is it cheating if the religion lets the cheater say he's Christian?

5. What good is belief in a doctrine unable to prevent cheating?

6. Why does a religion not preventing cheating say it's reformative?

7. Is a doctrine reformative if unable to prevent cheating?

8. Should the unreformed cheater blame the religion for it?

9. Should the religion blame the cheater for not reforming?

10. Why isn't the religion effective enough to put an end to cheating?

Anyone answering these ten questions will begin to understand that religious indoctrination is far from rational, and religion not as good a moral preceptor as it was seventeen centuries ago. Moral precepts, to be effective, must fit the times. Nicene Christianity, in all its long experience, hasn't learned this. It now contributes nothing to its believers and other people that rational common sense can't do better. Were its religious promises and dogmas not preventing independent free thinking, in a generation or two from now the majority of the world's peoples would be living contentedly, even happily. If people devoted to independent thinking the time they now waste praying, soon everything that makes life worthwhile would come true—and with far less effort than today.

THAT OLD BOGY, FEAR

Fear of any kind is the number one enemy of reason. The Western individual, when he speaks of fear, only rarely if ever realizes how much he contributes to the prevalence of one of its most insidious varieties: the fear of an imagined God. Man's intelligence is in many respects amazing, but so is his naïveté when he, unthinkingly believing something he hears, depends on it more than on his own judgment. He then behaves in accord with what he has been told, not intelligently as he otherwise, normally, would. In the Western nations this happens to him as a matter of traditional practice. Almost as soon as a child learns to say "mama," it also hears the word "god"—and though quickly learning to associate pleasurable happenings with words like "mama" and "papa," it as rapidly learns to couple with the word "god" the occasional unacceptableness of its behavior and, at times, the unpleasant experiencing of pain. It persists in memory when the mother, saying "My God" or "God, look what you've done" or such, at the same time administers a spank to its buttocks—before straightening up the mess the child stirred up.

By this and other, calculated, means, *God* has become a household word as well as a commonly used expletive, but only because of the grip on the West by its religion: Christianity. And at about the time the child ought to be learning the facts of the matter—by hearing from its parents that the word is a hangover: the result of the Western peoples' indulgence of ancient but now exploded superstitions—it is one nice Sunday packed off to where children are told that the word so familiar to its ears represents an *existing* something: God.

This, though at first astounding news, the child along with others five or six, learns to accept as valid fact. Why not—hasn't all this been told it by that proper Sunday school teacher: an adult who "knows"? And so Sunday after Sunday the child's indoctrination progresses until every bit of the nonsense of superstitious religionism becomes part of its developing personality. The tragedy in this farce is that for at least a long time when not for the duration of their lives it prevents every one of those growing tots from speculating about and seeking for the possibly determinable meaning to itself of life, and to life of itself. Each child this way becomes unknowingly a slave to ideas conceived for it by someone else.

In this manner the child's indoctrination in our Nicene Christianism terminates with its mind all jammed with concepts of heaven and hell, along with other dogmas of whatever sect its parents expose it to. If this isn't injustice then it certainly is a colossal blunder. Every generation this way "educates" the next one to react to fear throughout its days till death, and to unprotestingly, even devoutly, accept it as though it were a systemically unavoidable component of human existence. The brainwashed individual only rarely comes to realize that this which happened, happened of artifice, and that he has been duped. When he doesn't, the fear eats away inside his mind like the worm in an apple, usually for life leaving him with his mentality in a state of narcotized mediocrity.

In the Western world's cities and hamlets, from palace to hovel, first the parents and, next, trained religious workers impose this yoke upon the young—upheld in it by nearly everybody because everyone has had the habit imposed upon him that same way. It is a vicious circle. We could view this ridiculous situation as a hugely malicious joke played by the Fates on the West if at the same time it weren't so harmful, and causing trouble which it is pressingly important we correct. Fear of this kind, if it doesn't produce an inhibitive effect on the normal thinking and latent talents of man, certainly wastes the time he expends in coping with it. In fear of God, a few thousand years ago the Ammonites in propitiation considered ethical the sacrificing of infants to Molech; only four and five centuries ago we of the West burned heretics at the stake to preserve the potency of the fears innate in the Nicene Christian doctrine; and today hardly a soul deems reprehensible our sacrificing the sanity of outlook of entire generations of children for the subsistence of the selfsame Christianist dementia. This custom of ours is approved of by our authorities for the same reason that ancient authorities approved of theirs: for securing blind compliance.

Although these are less superstitious times, religious dogmatism still prevails, producing the same old desired result: keeping the people from thinking and reasoning. Two factors contribute to this. Most of the people don't give the matter the needed reflection, being too busy coping with the problems of making a living, and the rest are spellbound by the luxuries purchasable by the dollar. Anyhow—why think? It's hard work, and when anyone occasionally wonders about life and death, the old religious answers dispense with further thinking—the very result they were anciently conceived for. When the individual doesn't look into the validity of those answers, he is kept from discovering that his acceptance of them is actually responsible for much that in his life sorely irks him. As a result, when the average man asks his neighbor's opinion of this or that, the pat answer he gets is "God only knows." Trite, but it's the modern paraphrase of the ancient belief the witch doctors with an eye on gain for themselves succeeded in implanting. "God's watching your every move," the people were told—a sentence that, soon believed, was next amplified by the ascription to God of the priests' worst characteristic: vengefulness.

In the vengeful God the priesthood now commanded a haunting bogy which, after a bit of refurbishing, emerged from the fog of ancienty as our Judeo-Christian God—one who, they said, could and would avenge for your any transgression, and, sauce on the pudding, a God that, if you were "tempted" to feel free, as for example, to come to church only when you desired, or didn't respect and comply with sundry other religious dogmas, would consign you to the everlasting fires of hell. The believer is to this day given to understand that the only way to escape that God's ire is do whatever the Apostolic Successor, Bishop, or Pastor, commands—and even when he doesn't take it too seriously he, for the sake of approbation and peace, pays lip service to it because his sanctimonious or fanatically religious neighbors do.

That the priesthoods themselves pay little attention to their religious dogmas and precepts is ever since the days of Boccaccio proverbial, and well illustrated by the droll story of the padre who on a Friday enjoying a generous slice of ham was interrupted by a group of callers, all parishioners. How dared he eat meat on Friday, they asked. His reply, "Don't do as I do, do as I say," might get a laugh but isn't very funny, pointing out the hypocrisy of most of the officialdom of Christianism. All its members are astute men who, except for having a harder time bamboozling today's more intelligent humanity, are of the same stamp as the original group that in Nicaea in A.D. 325 formulated most of the spectral dogmas for controlling the unthinking—dogmas postulating not only what happens to anyone after he dies, but, also, what will befall anyone who here on earth will not do as they tell him. Out of that synod in Asia Minor emerged—besides its sanction of the Judaic Father-God, the martyr Son-Redeemer, and the all-pervading Holy Spirit—a new version of Jesus' mother, no longer to be known as the mother of a number of siblings Jesus among them, but now averred the Virgin Mother of God, having asexually (!) conceived Jesus via the agency of the Holy Spirit. Unable to find any record of the thinking that in the synod developed the Holy Spirit concept and its link with Mary, I lean toward thinking that it inductively materialized out of the old Greek myth of Leda and the Swan—in it Leda made the mother of Pollux by the God Zeus, he disguised as a cob swan. The Holy Spirit is in Christianist depictions of the Father, the Son, and the Spirit, a dove—a concept for the above and other purposes connoting greater delicacy than a swan. I've already alluded to the synod's astuteness, but now must add creativeness, for some of the Nicene Council's work must be seen as arising from most dumbfounding afflatus. However, inexplicable here is that whilst the Christian believer deems the Leda story pure fable, he takes the Christian paraphrase of it as the holy truth, incontrovertible testimony to the power of organized propagandizing and indoctrinating.

To me, Greek mythology is no less real, or unreal, but far more esthetically imaginative, than the mythology of Christianism. Both are interesting as phenomena of romantic thought—though the latter, the inferior of them, alone remains with its fears haunting Western life. It's astonishing, but not flattering to Western thinking, that the absurdities of Christianist origin persist largely respected today despite the disenchanting history of their employment by post-Nicene hierarchs who, with the apostolic shepherd's crook inherited from Peter upraised, sentenced to torture, burial alive, stoning to death, burning at the stake, etc., anyone whose reasoning aroused him to rebel against their fantastic dogmatism.

Of late days, the hierarchs' apologists have said the hierarchs did such things very regretfully, in their time only because obligated to (not mentioning to what or whom obligated). I'm moved to indignation when nowadays I chance to read one or another article lauding some individual or sect of organized Christianism; am I to suppose today's Christianism is worth praising, or defending, more than in their time were lauded the actions of the Inquisition? Which is the more outrageous, the Inquisitor's killing of heretics, or the force-feeding of Christianist nonsense killing the normality of millions of minds? On what grounds do today's religious dogmas deserve praising—dogmas today the same and as stultifying as they were in the Dark Ages? Because Christian indoctrination postulates that fear alone is able to hold the "sinful and bestial" human in check? Have all of us forgotten the power for good innate in our conscience, cultivatable by means of education?

An interesting difference between Christianism and various Eastern religions exists in that the latter need no modernizing because in them Deity is a concept acceptable as much to reason as to superstition. Most such theosophies deem their Deity or Deities in one or another way related to man. *They,* nota bene, encourage the believer to become not a blind idolater but a thinking, speculating, seeker of possible truths. There's a marked disparity between any religion of that kind and Christianism. Christianity forbids him to entertain any thoughts about God other than those it prescribes. *They* challenge him to fearlessly try penetrating the riddle of *is*ness—that way teaching him to appreciate the marvelous interaction of cosmic forces. *They* do not command but invite. *They* do not threaten him. *They* thus appeal irresistibly to man's instinctive desire to be at peace with all of creation.

To my way of thinking, all religions are redundant, this of course excluding ethical *philosophies* such as those of Confucius and Mencius. But, hung up on religion as the West is, what a boon it would be were it to profess belief in a religion not commanding, as Christianism does, that the believer not do this or that because the Bible says so—a pretense holding the Bible to be a repository of infallible truths beyond the pale of diacritical examination or man's complete understanding. The difference between Eastern religions and ours is that the former attempt to condition man to understand life on the basis of participative, cogitative humility; the latter, ours, insisting that only by obeying its dogmas will the believer be able to escape the wrath of Jehovah.

Every Christian sect today is far more concerned about its flock's belief as materializing, after services, in the vestry's tiller than in the congregation's belief in its superstitious dogmas and precepts. The byword is that whoever brings money, *believes.* Having long now relegated the hows and whys of moral ethics to a minor place in church affairs, all the major Christian sects and sub-sects should expect their decline. Only one or two of them have any excuse for existing such as before A.D. 325 prompted anyone to embrace Christ's precepts. Practically all of the sects are beguiled by the lustre of coinage, are cluttered with property and obsessed with and committed to amoral activities, although committed—they tell us—to worship. They've fallen prey to the very sins Christ preached against. The bigger and richer any church nowadays, the more hypocritical, bigoted and pagan its congregation.

Every particle of today's Christianism is blind to the demands of the times—not only because failing to recognize that *its own salvation* rests in its cultivation of a rational outlook, but, even when toying with that idea, in yet employing for it an outworn, fear-laden method. The existence of mankind manifests that life on earth is dynamized by the rays of our sun, and most of today's Western people, except rabid churchgoers, are more than half convinced it is fact. This is a new era indeed, requiring that man cultivate a rationale enabling him to face the facts of life unafraid. Were he informed in that way by means of rational education, he'd gain a lot more spiritual satisfaction and peace of mind out of his sojourn on earth than out of the religious nonsense he only half respects today. Even the man whom we call "bad" would undoubtedly be more easily rehabilitated morally by recourse to sound sense than by the methods we now employ.

Today's Christianism, fortunately for our future behavior, affects us much less than it affected our forebears. If our times, now, aren't times of Christianist decay then, surely, this scientifically minded period calls for an ethic formulated and cultivated by educational authorities without any resort to the bogus fear of God. The future is always malleable, it is said, but the maul shaping it must be swung with plenty of muscle and properly directed. For this the God bogy is useless; no valid evidence exists of theophany. This notwithstanding, there's no good reason why anyone who believes in a God shouldn't worship Him. However, I must insist that man's respect for an ethic directing his behavior should never be promoted through the worship. Worship and ethicality are two entirely distinct matters. This is irrefutable when we consider that people who do not worship a God are every whit as moral as those who do.

OF CHRISTIANIST FOLLY

One of the most insidiously spirit-quenching, inhumane and inhibitive of Christianity's dogmas, but paradoxically the most profitable for its business, is the one postulating that man is weak, susceptible to temptation and therefore of a fundamentally evil disposition—but that all this he can overcome by turning to Christ. Were this nonsense about human nature true, the nonchristian two-thirds of the world's population—informed about this boon-in-abeyance—would certainly rush to get converted. The missionary believes the rush hasn't materialized because the word hasn't gotten around as widely as it should. That most of the world's people might not care to be "saved" that way is a thought that, biased as he is, I'm almost sure hasn't yet occurred to him. That's why he is so hard to discourage from spreading "the great good news" wherever he is permitted to interfere. He usually goes preaching his religionary bit there where people exist in the most pitiful circumstances, getting the word accepted in trade for a bit of ordinary assistance that ought to be rendered, wherever and whenever needed, on purely humane grounds. But most inexplicable is how two out of every three people on the face of the globe have managed to exist for almost seventeen centuries since Nicene Christianity's advent without the doctrine that evangelism says is indispensable for everyone's good.

It seems to me irrefutable than man is gregarious, friendly, natively charitable, sympathizing and, though in many ways audacious, when not interfered with by do-goodybodies, nicely and completely humane. He has a talent for many things, most of them commendable. By now he would have attained in those qualities of his an unprecedented level had his instinctive cerebral drive—which everyone should roundly respect as his precious and inviolable endowment—not been brazenly interfered with by misanthropically conceived denigrations part and parcel of today's Christianistic indoctrination. The variety of ideation with which in the West practically every child's impressionable mental constitution is assaulted and adulterated is to my mind an unforgivable, stupendously insolent crime against humanity committed by Christianity.

Christian theosophy is replete with irrational fantasies. These would be in part excusable were they to be confined to the religion's esoteric variety of worship—for anyone to accept or reject—but the religion imposes them on the Western people when they are young and helpless to protest, presenting its postulates as a dependable guide for life. Christianism is arrogantly tricky, hammering away about its infallible wisdom at everyone's superstitious tendencies from his childhood on. Not only victimizes it those whom it embroils in its tentacles of unreason, but is itself victimized by its own delusive promises—just like the salesman who falls for the other salesman's pitch if it resembles his own.

One after another, the religion's hierarchs have over the centuries become so confident of the potency of their mind-stultifying elixir, they're not about to change any more than are its lay defenders. Both of them claim, whenever their religious doctrine is opposed, that only insensitive and narrow minds insist on a rational explanation of the faith's miraculous character. But when they choose to pontificate philosophically, they tell us those very same minds are insensitive and narrow if they take anything for granted. The American Indian brave would say that's talking with a forked tongue. The gambler calls it dealing from the bottom of the deck. I call it duplicity, deception, lying. But no matter: the loyal believers help perpetuate it by supporting it fiscally.

A fair sample of the deceptive hokum that theism has for centuries been getting away with presents itself in Roman Catholicism. There a married couple are told that in coition they mustn't use contraceptives. This of course invites pregnancy at best resulting in irresponsible childbearing. Even so, the couple—having observed the religion's orders—deserve hearing that everything now is first rate: good. But no such luck. They're in more trouble, once the two become three, than before. The Church—having bulled the couple into doing and having what they may or may not have desired—now ordains that their infant was born of sin, which means that the coition, and the way prescribed for it by the religion, leading to the birth of their child, was despicably sinful: evil.

Such double-dealing scandalizes moral sensibilities, will corrupt any prerational mind. It also warns anyone looking to the day when rational precepts will replace religious dogmas that he'd better be patient. The religiose wizard will certainly try to contrive whatever will put that day off. It could be something even more fantastic than the "virgin conception" he's made so many believe brought into the world the Christ whom in the fourth century the organizers of the wizard's Nicene Christianism prestidigitated into "The Son of God." Who can predict what a religious enthusiast will think of next?

In the God Business anything goes so long as done in the name of God, including prating about holiness but doing the opposite. But every sect nevertheless claims being a respectworthy, if not trustworthy, moral guide. Christianism is miraculous; it's a veritable miracle that, crammed with such follies, it has managed to survive till now. Most of its enouncements make no sense, but it knows where it is trending—at all times toward keeping everyone from thinking. The moral problems today facing us call for clear analysis of their causes. If religion is the lone way to their solution, be sure there are dozens of religions offering greater opportunity for clear thinking than the Christian doctrine for centuries, as now, preventing rational consensus in the Western world.

A rational method of study of and inquiry into the fundamentals of human behavior would repair the damage already done. Every school should include in its program the subject of moral ethics, encouraging the young from childhood on to speculate why one kind of behavior is called right and another wrong. The new generations would this way learn what the two embrace and entail by way of action and consequences. Once launched, the teacher would enter the studies only were it to become evident that the student was possibly misunderstanding the essence of the subject. As of now, not only do we have no such curriculum, but do no more than give the student an arbitrary good or bad mark for behavior—and that only for his behavior in classes. The subject in some of our schools called *Citizenship* regiments the student, indoctrinates him to respect traditional shibboleths. He isn't encouraged, let alone permitted, to question or speculate. Up to this time our educational methods have aimed at accomplishing the very thing the young so resent: making them docile parrots repeating outworn homilies. They're to be commended when they rebel; shouldn't be demeaned for it. It conclusively proves that much needs changing, and that the new generations are more alive to this than the old.

INQUISITIVENESS

Thinkers, teachers, originators, founders. In these and other types of the creative mind, one trait is common to all—inquisitiveness. Christ was a thinker and exceedingly inquisitive. Had he not been, he wouldn't have perceived and resented the injustices of his time, nor would he have attacked them as he did. We know he left home in his teens and returned when thirty. Those fifteen years; a half of his life, are a blank—where he went, what he did there is unknown. But where, in those days, could one go but eastward? He came home matured, experienced, full of ideas and plans for liberating the people of his native land from the Roman yoke. Matthew, Mark, Luke, and John tell us he talked much about "our Father in heaven"; but this is why until almost the end he wasn't suspected of gathering supporters for his political ideas. His great contribution to intellectual and political freedom (for which he deserves far greater acclaim than for being, as is said, "the Son of God") was his, then radical, idea that anyone, even the humblest slave or criminal, could himself appeal directly to God and, having made the effort, get a hearing.

Saul of Tarsus brought this radical message to the northern shores of the Mediterranean shortly after Christ's death, three hundred years *before* what we call Christianity was first organized. The message, as I will show, initiated the fall of Roman colonialism. How? Up until then any appeal to Rome's Gods could be made only through the head of one's own family—its head jealously guarding his privilege, fully aware that this was what kept all Roman households, underlings and slaves, under control. Christ's idea thus threatened to destroy the foundations supporting Rome's solidarity and power. Christ, a native of one of Rome's vassal provinces, surely knew what his idea represented. He didn't live to see its consequences. For the next three hundred years Christ's idea kept in constant turmoil not only the common people, but as well the Roman citizens and patricians along the entire perimeter of the Mediterranean. The authorities then forestalled a general revolt by calling Christ's idea religious hysteria, and by burying it within a hurriedly organized theism in many ways resembling the

Inquisitiveness

Roman which, not long after, they proclaimed the empire's official religion.

As ever, greed now appeared on the scene in the persons of astute Nicene patriarchs. They of course perceived that the individual's direct appeal to God was depriving them of the status previously enjoyed by the heads of the Roman households. A changeover now took place, the individual was commanded to go to church where, if he observed official church dogmas, the priest now interceded for him with the same old God who, Christ said, could be appealed to all on one's own. In this way, between A.D. 313 and 380, in Nicaea, Jerusalem, Constantinople, Athens, Alexandria, and of course Rome, was Christianity politically organized, and on that basis being administered today. I dare say were Christ to see what Christianity turned out to be that he'd despise it. But the authorities and their priests erred in thinking that Christ's idea was safely buried in the newly-dug religious grave. It stayed alive. A mere century later, all of this, done to save Roman supremacy, failed. Rome fell, and its might existed only in memory. Now, buried in the gloom of Christianity, all that remains of Christ's hope for human freedom is a faint spark awaiting someone as bold as he was to blow it aflame.

What is to be done? The Christian religion, a travesty on the honesty, unselfishness, and benevolence the word *Christ* reminds one of, is a fact impossible to ignore. Grown fat, lazy, and sprawling from addiction to the very things it tells us are evil, make it a moral monstrosity. Today's realist sees it a colossus of self-contradictory, morally flavored, didactic anecdotes submerged in tinselly pomp and cabalistic ritual, pretentiously theistic and spiced with extras appealing to superstition—morally almost useless. It is grandiose mummery, which today's mentally unshackled human thinks anyone should be able to live decently and happily without. Alone the arrogant pretensions of those in it who say they are Vicars of Christ on Earth are enough to repel any reasoning individual, making him thankful for the inquisitive faculties enabling him to distinguish between the true and the false.

Some of the concepts Christians believe in, and are by the cleric continually assaulted to keep on respecting, are comparable to the concept of "ether wind." In 1887 Michelson and Morley conducted experiments which proved that "ether wind" was pure delusion. Until then most of the respected men of science mistakenly believed it fact. The big difference between men of religion and men of science, of course, is that the latter tentatively entertain cogent theories and postulates until disproved, but the religious keep right on calling true what sometimes a thousand years ago was conclusively proved false.

Patient inquisition into all aspects of life is the best, and possibly the only, reason the realist can give for existence—and in this our only hope of ever finding something truly dependable to believe in. We are a gullible lot. The lack of an answer to one or another demand of our curiosity is a poor excuse for calling it holy. To do so is not only invalid but, ethically, evil. Shooing people into believing sundry unprovable religious hypotheses is the same as saying that ignorance is Divine. But to anyone who says God exists it seems proper, I suppose, that anything equally unprovable should also be called His.

Such reasoning, though having an outcome, is not only fatuous but destructive to the intellect. In the Western world it is a well established bad habit employed for the eliciting of wishful conclusions. To believe in a Deity conceived as a substitute for cogent answers to inquiry is certainly not wise, nor is it sane to expect any so conceived God to ever materialize. Last of all, to believe that a God this way conceived of human ignorance actually exists, as so many believe, is an insult to any conjecturable God who would or could care to be interested in the problems of the mold called humanity infesting the surface of Earth, it a mere speck among countless superior bodies in the Universe—many of which might, for all we know, be infested by a mold of an immensely more advanced type.

In matters like the above the painter of canvases and the preaching cleric have at least one thing in common. Both aim to obtain a response from the sensibilities of their audience. The artist does it with pictures and the cleric with promises. The cleric claims his promises are truth from the lips of (an unperceivable) God, saying that to be "redeemed" you must believe his words represent God's opinion on the subject and so accept it. This, if you are a believer you do—and because originally the cleric made a believer of you, it is he and not God who decides for you. You had no choice in the matter. The painter, his picture an abstract of the reality we all perceive exists, usually looks forward to his next canvas, hoping to do better. You don't have to like his picture, but whether you do or not, you yourself make the decision, not the artist. You had free choice. So, although the aims of the cleric and the artist are similar, the response obtained by each of them is of opposite value. This should remind us that similar aims don't always produce similar results—and to think twice before taking for granted that dogmas represent the holy truth.

The individual who believes that freedom, of thought, expression and action is to be highly prized should view anything "holy" with circumspection if not suspicion. The "holy" always comes in a handsomely wrapped package tied with an occult ribbon and bow. He should undo it and find out what's inside. The package is made up so cleverly for inducing him to buy it without looking—and to make him either contribute materially or dispossess himself intellectually—or both—for the benefit of those who that way perpetuate a phantasm conceived and intended for immobilizing everyone who has or could have an abiding desire to see the world made into a place where mankind would exist free of all haunting bogies. We live only once, an experience much too precious to trade to an astute mountebank for his package of barefaced lies—a package which, once we've bought it, will enable him to do with our bodies and minds as he might please.

But for the vendors of "holiness," everyone could experience a life so pleasant and in every way bountifully rewarding that after reaching a ripe age he'd little regret facing his last day. This almost elysian kind of life is available to anyone *un*willing to be fooled. Abraham Lincoln's remark about fooling the people still holds good today. Some can be fooled, but not all of them all of the time. Unfortunately, most people are so busy with the pressing matters of daily life they rarely inquire into and challenge the validity of religious promises. Fortunately, though, due to modern communications, little by little but perceptibly, the results of man's native inquisitiveness are on the upgrade, Christianistic postulations to the contrary notwithstanding.

"HE DIED FOR OUR SINS"

The doctrine of Christianism is stuffed to bursting with overweening claims and wearying rhetoric. It is difficult to understand why those interested in the ascendancy of the religion hadn't rid it of these superfluous trappings one by one, in keeping with each forward step in world intellect. Had Christianity done this, the West wouldn't be in the position of needing to accept penalties today for its third-rate intellectuo-spiritual attitude at the hands of those to whom it purveys its first-rate technology. The technologically backward Eastern nations, far ahead of us philosophically, but customers of the West, throw their hands up in dismay when asked to accept the extras, the reservations, that we insist go with any projected sale; with every million we lend for rehabilitation goes its quota of missionaries. They want none of the West's Christianistic sophistry. Why should they?

One of Christianism's prime postulations is that man is born of sin and is a sinner, and that Christ died on the cross to expiate those sins. This tale, a good two-thirds of it originally fabricated for the purpose of driving the listener into the net of those who then profited from it (as those who today propagate it do) wasn't effective enough to begin with; it was consequently embellished, becoming an ode in which Christ was elevated into being the literal Son of God—this in order to dramatize his death as a death of an exceptional kind.

"The Son of God died for your sins," they keep on telling us sanctimoniously, forgetting the millions who died as permanently since Christ's crucifixion, in useless, wasteful and brutal wars, for the sins of omission and commission perpetrated by the nations of the West whose guiding lights proudly call themselves Christians. The Son of God protects our boys on the battlefield, people of each side tell us. That Christ in most instances is said to have called himself *Son of man* is of no avail in reviewing his status with his exponents—Christ's divinity, in all Christian sects, is a subject closed to all discussion. It is reasonable to assume that Christianism will one day rue this Christ-God concept it dreamed up so long ago.

"He Died for Our Sins"

To ascribe to Christ that he believed his death would expiate the sins of his own people, people alive in his time, is not too unreasonable; religious zealots died for lesser convictions. But that Christ could think that he was dying in expiation of all the imaginable sins that the hundred generations of all the world's nations committed after his time until this day is, to put it mildly, somebody's dream stuff. And that he was so egocentric as to believe that his death on the cross could cleanse all the people of all coming generations of their sins is a premise that only a theologian could be expected to defend. Were Christ to have believed all this about himself it would certainly have distinguished him as the most grandiose swell-head in all history. And to top that, the sinners are multiplying! Today there are twice as many sinners on the globe as occupied it in 1900. Three billions of them, in various camps, and all at each other's throats.

Deaths in battle in World War I totalled about 15,000,000 and about the same number in World War II. Every one of those men died for, and because of, sins committed by the people of the nations for whose "honor and integrity" each fought. Just think, 30,000,000 individual agonizing deaths all within the span of only 30 years! Every one of those men died because he and the other people of those warring nations weren't convinced—by the precepts that besainted Christianity says make men better (forgetting to say better than what)—that they should conduct themselves decently. Of those 30,000,000 deaths, approximately 20,000,000 were deaths of men of opposite Christian nations. Thus actually Christians were killing one another! What a gruesome testimonial all those crosses on graves make for Christianism! And all for naught; the world is worse off now, morally, than before. There are no words meaningful or capacious enough to describe behavior so stupid, so idiotic, so revolting. And you want Christianity respected? For what? In view of such carnage, what has it contributed; what does it amount to?

An ethic is made defunct when, besides saying that authorities who foment wars break God's sixth, eighth, and tenth commandments, it postulates that Christ, by his dying, atoned for such sinning if the warmakers afterwards go to church and confess they're sorry. Such an ethic is morally as culpable as are the warmakers themselves. How can anyone believe that Christ, in his day a keenly progressive thinker and humanitarian, could have been so stupid as to sacrifice himself in order to excuse such premeditated criminality? It's unthinkable; unthinkable, that is, for anyone except those still mesmerized by Nicene dogmatism. "He died for our sins" confirms wishful thinking, a poor substitute for thinking of the rational kind.

Today's unthinking masses react to that wishful dogma the same as they have from the time it first appeared. But when war comes home today to the millions who've lost their sons and daughters in it, and also to noncombatants exposed to aerial bombing of "strategic objectives," the crucifixion of Jesus doesn't seem nearly as dramatic as it did before Christianity learned how to kill in wholesale lots. Oughtn't we suppose that every father and mother who lost a son in those wars, the kids who lost their fathers, and the others who lost their kin, all subconsciously feel that their dead gave up their lives for the sins of the world? Did Jesus do more?

Maybe, but only maybe, he did. His concept that every man, rich or poor, emperor or slave, could speak directly to God was something revolutionary—two thousand years ago. That concept of his, about man's right to be heard by God without the intercession of a middleman, was responsible for the wrecking of the far-flung Roman empire. Jesus said that you, or anyone, can speak directly to God. Do, if you wish to. But those who now consider The New Testament an authority will not find it confirming, as so many take for granted, that Jesus said he was "the only begotten Son of God, sent to die so all might gain everlasting life." That statement could have been made only by those who saw that its drama would command wide attention useful for attracting additional converts to their fledgling religion.

What kind of a God could it be who would sacrifice his son to save the mankind that (as says the Christian) the God himself created? Wouldn't it be a stupid God that would create something as imperfect as man, just so he could sacrifice his son to save it? So, the next question is: Can you believe God would play such games? And if Jesus thought that by the simple act of his dying he'd expiate the sins of all mankind—wouldn't you think that he'd have to presume that his life was worth all the others? And in such a case—if he were the Son of God, the God who sent him here to die—don't you think he'd think Father was overdoing things?

All in all, the entire business of Christianism is one thoroughgoing tragicomedy. All of it boils down to a series of conjectures that, when shed, makes a person feel clean and decent and ready to face life with a brain ready and avid for solving the problems of life. It's like awakening from a bad dream—out of a nightmare.

The moral disintegration and internecine confusion today rampant in the world is to a great extent the result of myriad conflicting religious dictums and the consequent quarreling over them. These disparate dictums and beliefs prevent all men, of all the nations and races, from emerging upon the enlightened plateau of brotherhood, a plateau upon which one day—when they come to their senses—all will trust one another and live together peaceably. Obviously, these dictums preventing peace in the world aren't philosophically adequate; if they were, the world would be an ideal place for everybody to live in.

What is needed for peace in the world is not more of the Christianity that made the Westerner into what he is, but less of it—and more of something able to supply him with a more effective variety of moral guidance—guidance that will enable him to realize *why* decency is worth practicing. He must be shown to himself for what he is, not what Christianity has led him to imagine himself to be; he must be taught of what he comprises as man. He must learn to understand what makes him tend to harm himself and others and learn how to overcome it. This, in a few generations would impel him to conduct himself as he now should —he would then be working for his own as well as the common good.

The world, especially the Christian Western world, needs a new and much better teacher of moral ethics than its Christianism. Needed here is an ethic that the individual will be able to depend on and unreservedly trust, to keep himself and his fellowman, during their lifetimes, creatures able to face themselves without any risk of revulsion and loss of self-respect. Be sure, the

Westerner nowadays betrays much that adherents of other religions and different ideologies shun him for.

Before man solves the problem of being equitably sheltered, fed, and clothed, he must first be protected from false advice. And now that in many nations he has leisure time, devote some of it to speculating about a world where existence would be a lot more pleasant than today. In such a world—were all men in it of rational outlook—he could live at peace with himself. But after speculating this way he'd soon conclude that a world of people of rational outlook can't exist while depending on Christianism for its moral guidance. Christianism, having made the West what it morally is, is here just as elsewhere each day less credible. Ever since its inception seventeen centuries ago, and all that time promising but failing to deliver what it promised to each succeeding generation, its credibility is close to zero. It would probably have long yet remained unchallenged as a teacher of its kind of morality, had circumstances not forced the people of today's materialistic era, more knowledgeable than those who lived when Christianism was born, to realize its shortcomings.

Having a better teacher, everyone would realize that no imaginary God wards off harm; that rational judgment alone, one's own, can. There'd be no cheating for selfish gain then; no panicking terror prompting people to kill one another in imagined self-defense. Today even the common man doubts that his prayer to his God will have much effect—he is beginning to perceive its futility. He now needs protection from the religious tampering that interferes with his awareness of the realities of existence, and his natural aptitude for dealing with them. Nature, after all is said and done, isn't an enemy of life, but, when understood, its friendly sustainer. So, for him to be taught to pray to a spectral God for help in this or that (and, as he still does: for things as stupid as victory in battle against his fellowman) ranks him, by way of intelligence, alongside his cavedweller ancestors.

Let those who can't depart from praying to God thank Him only for their life. Any sane God would turn down thanks for anything else, although, on second thought, He might promptly attend to the plea that He deliver all of humankind from the hell visited on it by the misanthropic dogmas of the God Business.

OF ORIGINAL SIN

It appears reasonable to respect the conclusion that the lives of all people are shaped by three factors: first, inherited talents and tendencies; second, their education; third, that what any individual in question happens to contact or be confronted by throughout his life, namely: experience.

Every human being is to a degree capable of meditation and in this his native capacity and its quality depend, to some extent, upon his immediate progenitors and progressively less upon his ever more remote antecedents. Until recent times modern man has had but little time to think, even when inclined to, but now the average man is being afforded more and more leisure for thinking than ever before.

Like nearly everyone nowadays, I'm aware through personal experience of the intensity with which the cult of modern business and technology worships work, but I tend to believe that most people who hate but devote themselves to their work do it because their occupations reflect their idea of the least exertion for value received. People this way believe they attain the most leisure at least cost to themselves. This is more or less true about people at large even when they aren't consciously aware of their behavior or of the opportunities for thinking that leisure offers them.

Whether people take leisure to mean indolence or surcease from labor, once attaining it they are bound to arrive at the doors opening to the provinces of contemplation—and begin thinking about one matter or another. Sooner or later, they'll hit the big question: "It's not too bad a world but how did it all begin?" Then starts the fun.

When such a philosopher begins to think about the biblical version of creation it's never very long before his thoughts hit the barrier of Christianity's original-sin concept. Because up to then he didn't have time to think about this, and because by his indoctrination into Christian thinking he is practically prevented from thinking clearly, he needs help and encouragement.

Basically, of course, the psychotic concept of sin was introduced in the West by the Hebraic concept of original sin postulated in Genesis. But try to rationalize this away if you can: How it is possible for an innocent, helpless babe to be culpable and responsible, as the Bible implies, for the actions of its parents—remembering, besides all else about it that we have been told, that the "stigma" is transferable?

Bibliolatrous logic premises on the assumption that anything done by two "sinning" people, male and female, concludes in a sinful outcome: a child marked by the "sin." I can't go along with those who call procreation "sinning," nor with what Christianity postulates: that the child is now culpable to an extent requiring it to beg God's forgiveness for having been born. In Christianity's view the child, as soon as born, is an incipient sinner, from then on requiring constant stewardship by Christian priests. How in the name of reason could such a thing be credible, let alone possible? Yet multitudes today take this for God's truth! Why they believe it is no moot question because we know that the concept was funneled into them long before they were able to think for themselves. What a travesty on life and truth it is, to instruct a trusting tot that its parents sinned when they conceived it, and (now try to stomach *this*) that, because of its parents' alleged sinning, it itself is a sin-damned creature! Can any mind that conceived such putrid thoughts be deemed anything but malevolent? Can truth be tortured more? What, in religion, is there that is as inspirational, as ecstatic, as superterrestrial, as the love shared by a decent male and female—love the poets sing of; call it sex or whatever?

Original sin! Original sin! Why doesn't Christianism, whose Bible says that God created us endowed with sexuality, consider *Him* the sinner? When, as Genesis avers, God set male and female together in Eden, couldn't He anticipate what even a fool knows would surely happen? Was that God of the Bible experimenting or just playful? Why doesn't the Bible say, and the Christian believe, that all known life is to be deemed culpable for reproducing itself?

To our best knowledge, the only creature able to respond to the doctrine of original sin, and its consequently debilitating fear of God, is man; and he falls for it only because he has an insup-

Of Original Sin

pressibly lively imagination: connoting intelligence. So there's nothing very strange about the unthinking when they fear a dreamed-up God; nor is it anything but an awakening from a daze when some of them begin wondering whether or not their fears of a God make sane sense. It's an unmistakable sign of man's latent capacity to distinguish between right and wrong when he begins distrusting anyone as indifferent as Jehovah—as the Bible shows Jehovah was—about all that was injuring His favorite people *before* their actual departure from Egypt. Just think what later troubles, He, omnipotent, could have spared them then, by moving only a whisker. These and sundry other fables that in the Bible conjure up fears of a God attest that in those ancient times the leaders of the people already knew that such fears would make the people docile. Moses used every artifice of this kind to make his wandering tribe manageable. But today is *now*: an era many thousand years later. So let no mind misunderstand why Christianity is chock-full of allusions to a vengeful God. The very word *religion* derives from the Latin *religio,* meaning *taboo* and *restraint.*

It is beyond valid contradiction that decent behavior benefits everyone, and that ethical rules promote this. But in this day it's altogether ridiculous to believe that the effectiveness of such rules should depend on the fear of a hypothetical God's punishment. Inasmuch as an ethic superior to any basing on fear is readily available (if only schools would teach the young the benefits of decency in human relations), it's obvious why so many people—even though they constitute but a minority today—consider it stupid to respect behavioral rules based on the fear of a God of whose existence no one has any factual evidence. These people live by a code of rational devising: an ethic cognizant of the facts of life—one respecting the prerogatives of their fellowmen.

Today, in full view of this, it's amazing that churchgoers remain so supine: keeping coming back to hear the cleric tell them they're sinners. Were the precepts the pastor repeats effective, then, once heard, there would be no need for the congregation to come back.

Despite this presently sad state of our spiritual outlook, we of the West have advanced far enough, reasonwise, to devise an ethic stripped of religious folderol such as "original sin." Once we will have willed to do this, it will benefit not only us, the people and nations of the West, but, moreover, gain us the respect of the people of all the other nations of this planet, facilitating harmonious relations in the work crying to be done for the preservation of the human race.

THE RADIO EVANGELIST

Nearly all people young and old nowadays listen to the radio. An almost miraculous medium of communication, radio is around-the-clock full of chatter of diverse quality about subjects of all kinds. Most of the sermonizing called Evangelism and over the air aimed at the listeners deserves being called monologic drivel —though some of the listeners of my acquaintance tell me they think it highly entertaining if taken with a pinch of salt, or a dram or two. Those of us who've lived long enough to have been parts of the half-credulous assemblages listening to the histrionic harangue of the now extinct patent medicine salesman—a paragon of the appeal to the emotions, whose horsedrawn booth on wheels, and jars of snakes, a few score years ago ornamented and enlivened every county fair and chautauqua gathering—wax nostalgic and harken back to those days when hearing the evangelist of radio gospeldom, his modern counterpart. But there's a distinct difference between the two breeds. Whilst the oratory of the gospeller suffuses us with memories of county fairs in sunnier and more peaceful times, and though to some of us his ranting is amusing, the nostrum he sells is subversive—not at all like the medicine man's.

The harangues of the one just like the other were conceived to overcome the listeners' suspicions of all rosy promises and those who make them. And that old-time salesman knew just as well as today's evangelist how to handle incredulity. For my part, I think he understood the subject even better. Of the two, I'll take the old-timer any day. He made his spiel and for your money he at least delivered a bottle with something in it never harmful or poisonous. The evangelist makes his spiel and should you decide to buy you'll get nothing but promises. Should you believe his promises, a good part of your mind will never be the same as before. And until you come to your senses and again disbelieve him, you'll be the slave of phantasmagoria whose fleeting images he and you, together trying as hard as you might, will never be able to hold in mental focus long enough to substantively describe.

Try it—try describing to yourself that promised heaven of his. It will be revealing.

To my mind the wildest of the gospelmongers, who spouts from a Border station double the wattage of the highest in our land of the free and gappy communications—and whom I occasionally tune in on—usually opens up with a short statement, the only one that in his program is acceptable to reason. Delivered in a normal disarming voice, that's the end of it. He then rapidly departs from it, climaxing in a frenzy of hysterical screeching. He does this, I suppose, having found that his listeners take this for his being moved by and commanding supernatural power. This deludes them to believe that through him they'll certainly gain whatever favor each of them seeks from God. It's a great act you shouldn't miss, and it's free for just tuning in.

Listening to him or his less violent but as artful brethren of the radio lanes wouldn't irritate me near as much were it not evident that the sanctimonious palaver of all of them is a smoke screen concealing their shooting at but one bull's eye: an increase in the number of their contributing listeners so this religio-farcial activity won't fade from the airwaves. Were that to happen, the pack of them would have to look for some other equally as profitable employment or bid farewell to the life that evangelizing has accustomed them to. I'm not saying they're lazy; show biz is a very demanding life. But, should their big act on the air not be the purely mercenary effort I make it out, I'll welcome any evidence able to move me to view it in some other way.

It seems reasonable to anticipate that should radio evangelizing continue unbridled, it will create a revulsion for everything that in today's Christianism forfends sane thinking, and that way awaken in the majority of the people a desire for a realistic outlook on life. That's the one optimistic thing about it. Some of the air sermons at times still sound like the "old-time religion" of fifty or more years ago, but today all of them are directed—not as subtly as in the past, but more deftly and successfully—at their audiences' pocketbooks. And this notwithstanding that practically all of them outlandishly misinterpret the old concept of God and whichever Biblical passage the evangelist selects for serving as

The Radio Evangelist

his come-on. A new God, but still superstition.

Radio evangelists usually deliver their appeals in one of three basic ways. First, God the Merciful and Providing—an approach pandering to the sensibilities of the listeners who justify their belief in the religion on the basis of its material usefulness to them. Second, God the Prescient—an attempt at getting the Bible accepted as His Word prophesying the present and future of today's scientifically enamoured and gadget-daffy world. Third, God the Miracle Worker—a device for attracting the physically ailing, and employing a few of their number, who for the time being believe themselves made well through faith, as examples of the evangelist's power of intercession with God for effecting cures. Aside from that, matters are on the upgrade: largely unmentioned on the radio is the God to whose vengeance and retribution the Bible devotes numerous pages—an image that in the Middle Ages served the Holy Inquisition as justification for its execution of interfering dissenters critical of the religion's dogmas. Although a realist like myself sees all these radio goings on as nothing but pure artifice, the evangelists, each one in his way, manage to attract adherents and contributors. This, I think, is what between themselves they allude to as the Power of God.

Also, the effectiveness of radio coverage has proved unprecedentedly prestigious to them. The most significant example of how in the USA prestige indirectly accrues to their profession, is the much publicized worshipping conducted in the White House by clerics of one and another of the leading sects at the invitation of the Chief Executive. This can't be said harmful to either the business of the cleric or the purposes of anyone committed to politics. One way or another, it's good to know that the Chief this way indicates he doesn't consider his will supreme—I think supreme should be the will of a rationally disposed people—and it's comforting to see him sufficiently authoritarian to have God's Word brought him in the person of His representative the cleric. Maybe we should have a Secretary of Evangelism to keep a sharp eye in Washington on all such evangelizing before it affects even more than already it has our Senators and Congressmen. Most of the people I know and respect tell me that when listening to radio they turn to another program when the evangelist begins; but I stay just to hear what novel twist the resourceful pro in the pulpit has improvised for an even wider acceptance of his flimflam.

Although radio preaching borders on comedy, its existence is less a laughing matter than a soberingly serious, even tragic, situation. Should such wholesale lying, over public communications media, remain un-neutralized by education, it will end up in our being a nation of schizophrenics incapable of making rational decisions. This, since we now lack any other method of cultivating ethical conduct, and certainly not a rational one, will leave our sanctimonious nation without a single precept for sane behavior. What then? What else but anarchy?

As I mentioned, the broadcasting troubadours of religion are consummate showmen. If they weren't, not much attention would be paid their performances. So it's no surprise that they stack their chips on Barnum's surmisal that a sucker is born every minute. Their acceptance shows that even nowadays an article as discredited as superstition can be peddled at a profit. Of course one day even the people now being this way bamboozled will grow weary of it. The evangelist's archaisms and technique are slated for failure because religion, if it is to survive a while longer, will be able to only through the efforts of clerics now trying to change it—recognizing that in its present form it bypasses the most important matter in life: living itself. Were our Christianism to regain its former image, it could happen only were the intelligence of the majority of the West's peoples to drop below its historically known low of long ago. The religion, along with our civilization which supports it, would then soon go the route of the civilizations of the Egyptian, the Greek, and the Roman—but go more rapidly because it doesn't serve the needs of the West's people anywhere near as well now as the religions of those extinct civilizations served theirs.

Very few religions have ever shown any but grudging regard for the common man's intelligence and get-up. Most of them took man's patience for stupidity. The hierarchs of religion should have perceived, long before this day, that man would sooner or later begin speculating about religion's promises of post-terrestrial bliss,

The Radio Evangelist

and would take steps—before entering the promised pearly gates—to get a bit of something of that kind out of his life right here on earth. This is happening now: today's citizen is finally beginning to see that he'll have to get it himself—that religion will not help him to it. I agree. Religion will not, not even were it to be reconstituted out of the best that exists in all of the known theosophies; they're every one of them useless for making him a rationally thinking creature.

Whatever in man's outlook is rational he attained to in spite of his religious superstitions. All evangelists, and with a few exceptions all priests and clerics, today view this new outlook of their flocks as a threat to their livelihood. This now is their prime concern, the very thing that happens in any other business. The cleric, when his church pews show more wood than people—and the radio evangelist, when his mail starts falling off—don't worry about the benefits of religion their absent buyers are depriving their "souls" of, any more than the auto-maker, when his sales chart shows a dip, worries about "souls" being deprived of the benefits of his own brand of auto transportation. At such a time all businessmen get to work at overcoming sales resistance. The cleric is an astute businessman with his eye on the cash register, in this respect topped within the craft of religion only by the broadcasting evangelist. The radio evangelist is thus far doing very well, but remember that in his day so was the evangelist of patent medicine.

The radio evangelist is a phenomenon proving that we still exist on a neolithically intellectual level when comparing it with the level reached by our technology. Our indoctrination in the superstitious concepts of religion, constantly abetted by evangelism, has made us afraid to accept the responsibility of thinking clearly, fearlessly and realistically, about the problems of our life.

CONCLUSION

Broadly speaking, everyone arrives in this world with the makings of a conscience that, properly cultivated, will make the newcomer aware of his responsibilities to himself and others. The sure way to it is by means of education devoid of dogmatic beliefs, the educational methods sponsored by rationally disposed civil authorities. An ethic deserves its name only because it recognizes the benefits of right—good. Our Christianist ethic postulates as holy truth that good is rewarded and evil punished: a promise only accidentally realized—too many instances exist of good unrewarded and evil unpunished. When good is ignored and evil uncorrected, the condition indicates a breakdown in ethical behavior. And though in all lands the ethic of each is implemented by laws, the effectivenes of the ethic depends on law enforcement. When the laws stand unenforced by enforcement agencies who themselves are partisans of the ethic, no other conclusion is possible but that the ethic lacks convincingness.

This now is our predicament—the result of our sentimental attachment to an outworn tradition. Though everyone isn't alive to this—but because all nevertheless sense it—we now suffer the ills of irresolution. Until recent times all in authority believed, as many authorities still do, that religion is the best preceptor for establishing decent demeanor. Today, when public opinion issues from factual information more than ever before, the religious way is at long last being seen as anachronistic if not fundamentally wrong. I trust the preceding essays to have made clear why, especially in the spheres of education and government, realism should be given precedence over dogmatism; and rationality over sentimentality.